CAMBRIDGE
UNIVERSITY PRESS

CAMBRIDGE PRIMARY
Global Perspectives

Learner's Skills Book 3

Gillian Ravenscroft

CAMBRIDGE
UNIVERSITY PRESS

Shaftesbury Road, Cambridge CB2 8BS, United Kingdom

One Liberty Plaza, 20th Floor, New York, NY 10006, USA

477 Williamstown Road, Port Melbourne, VIC 3207, Australia

314–321, 3rd Floor, Plot 3, Splendor Forum, Jasola District Centre, New Delhi – 110025, India

103 Penang Road, #05–06/07, Visioncrest Commercial, Singapore 238467

Cambridge University Press is part of the University of Cambridge.

It furthers the University's mission by disseminating knowledge in the pursuit of education, learning and research at the highest international levels of excellence.

www.cambridge.org
Information on this title: www.cambridge.org/9781009354196

First published 2024

20 19 18 17 16 15 14 13 12 11 10 9 8 7 6 5

Printed in Malaysia by Vivar Printing.

A catalogue record for this publication is available from the British Library

ISBN 978-1-009-35419-6 Learner's Skills Book 3 Paperback with Digital Access (1 Year)
ISBN 978-1-009-35809-5 Learner's Skills Book 3 – eBook

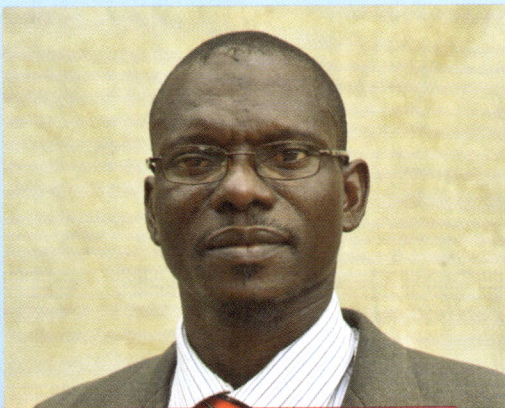

Endorsement statement

Contents

Introduction

Welcome to Stage 3 of **Cambridge Primary Global Perspectives**.
I hope you will find the projects in this book interesting.

You are going to work on four projects. The projects in this book help you to understand new things.

The projects are about:

- the way we travel
- the food we eat
- how people learn things
- the world's oceans.

You will have learning goals.

The learning goals help you know what to do.

There are four children in the book.

They try out all of the projects.

Here is Zara.

Here is Marcus.

Here is Arun.

Here is Sofia.

You do not need to learn facts.

You will need to help people.

You will learn how to:

- find out new facts
- find out what people think
- talk to lots of people
- think about what you do.

You will need to work in different ways.

- sometimes you will work on your own
- sometimes you will work with a partner or in a group
- sometimes you will learn in the classroom
- sometimes you will learn in different places.

There are lots of ways to do well:

- think about your own ideas
- think about other people's ideas
- try out new ways to learn
- help other people to learn new things.

I hope you will enjoy the projects in this book!

Gillian Ravenscroft

How to use this book

In this book you will find lots of different things to help your learning.

Activities at the start of a project to help you understand what you will be doing.

Getting started
1 Answer the questions with a partner: a What can you see in the picture?   b What kind of food and drinks do you think are best?   c Do all members of your family like the same kinds of food and drinks?   d How do people choose what food to buy in a supermarket?

What you will learn in the lesson. There is space for you to show what you think at the end of the lesson. There is also space for your teacher to say what you have learnt.

Learning goals

Our learning goals	I think	My teacher thinks
I can think about what happens when people do things and how their actions affect others.	★ ☺ ☹	★ ☺ ☹

This tells you what the key words are. Key words are in the glossary. The glossary is at the back of the book. You can find out what the key words mean there.

relevant

Activities to help you learn. →

How did we help each other in our group?

Arun and Sofia are thinking about how their group helped each other during the project.

It was really helpful looking at the map together – some of those learning places were not easy to find.

The rest of the group helped me make my information panel easier to understand.

1   Work with your group. Think about all the activities you have completed together. Talk about the things you did to help each other, then answer the questions.

Interesting facts and information. →

Did you know?

A lot of plastic is used only once before it is thrown away. We call it 'single-use plastic'. A plastic drinking straw is an example of single-use plastic. How many more examples can you think of?

**Useful words.
You can use these words.** →

drawing a picture   writing titles
attaching the labels   helping someone

Top tips. Advice to help you do the lesson. →

Top tip

Count the **tally** marks to find the answers to the questions. The tally marks are arranged in groups of 5 like this: ||||. You can count in 5s to make the counting easier.

🎧 Audio is available on Cambridge GO and in the Teacher's Resource.

🎥 Video is available on Cambridge GO and in the Teacher's Resource.

⬇ Your teacher will have access to free supporting resources through Cambridge GO – the home for all your Cambridge digital content.

How do we travel to school?

Getting started

Answer the questions with a partner:

a   What can you see in the picture?

b   How do you think Zara, Marcus, Sofia and Arun are feeling?

c   When cars and vans cannot move, we call it a *traffic jam*.
    Why do you think there is a traffic jam here?

d   Talk about your journey to school or another journey you take
    regularly. Is it like the one in this picture?

Marcus

driver

passengers

exhaust fumes

Zara

traffic

Sofia

Arun

pavement

van

> 1.1 How do we travel from place to place?

Learning goals

Our learning goals	I think	My teacher thinks
I can talk about why I do something and how it affects other people.	★ ☺ ☺	★ ☺ ☺ ....
I can describe what different people think about a topic.	★ ☺ ☺	★ ☺ ☺ ....

What happens in traffic?

1 You are going to watch a video about five different people who travel through the city every day. They are explaining how the traffic **affects** their journey.

> **affect**
> **get stuck in traffic**
> **courier**

Match each person to what they are thinking.

1 Pedro the van driver

2 Marta the office worker

3 Kesi the bus driver

4 Eryk the **courier**

5 Alisa the school child

a It's so boring when our car **gets stuck in traffic**!

b If I go too slowly, the food will get cold.

c I am worried that I'll be late for work.

d Customers will complain if their parcels arrive late.

e I don't want the children to be late for their lessons.

2 What other problems does the traffic cause for these five people?

3 Do the five people dislike the traffic for the same reason or for different reasons?

How does our journey to school affect others?

Read what Marcus has written about his journey to school.

> I travel by bus. It's fun when I can talk to my friends,
> but sometimes it's a bit boring if we get stuck in traffic.
> It is good for my parents because they don't have to drive me.
> Also, one bus takes less space than a lot of cars.

Think about your journey to school. Write the answers to the questions.

a   How do you travel to school? ....

....

b   How do you feel about your journey?

....

....

c   How does the way you come to school affect other people?

....

....

d   How does the way other people travel affect you?

....

....

Explain your answers to your partner.

Did you know?

Some children travel to school on a bicycle bus. One town in France calls this type of transport a 'S'cool bus'. That's a funny name!

What do we think about travelling to school?

1   Talk with your classmates. Do you all travel to school the same way? Which is the most popular way to travel to school?

2   Do all your classmates have the same opinion about travelling to school? Why do you think this is?

〉 1.2 How do children in our class think about travelling to school?

Learning goals		
Our learning goals	**I think**	**My teacher thinks**
I can make up my own questions to help me find out what people think.	★ ☺ ☺	★ ☺ ☺ ....
I can carry out a survey using my own questions.	★ ☺ ☺	★ ☺ ☺ ....

How can we find out what children think about travelling to school?

Zara and her group want to find out how children in their class think about their journey to school. They do a **survey**. Look at the results of their survey and answer the questions.

> **survey**
>
> **exhaust**
>
> **tally**

Questions about our journey to school	Yes	No	I'm not sure
Can children walk or cycle safely to our school?	‖‖ ‖‖	‖‖ ‖‖ ‖‖	‖‖ ‖‖
Are car journeys a safe way of travelling to our school?	‖‖ ‖‖ ‖‖ ‖‖	‖‖ ‖‖	‖‖‖‖
Is the amount of **exhaust** fumes on our journey to school too high?	‖‖ ‖‖ ‖‖‖‖	‖‖	‖‖ ‖‖ ‖

Top tip

Count the **tally** marks to find the answers to the questions. The tally marks are arranged in groups of five like this: ‖‖. You can count in fives to make the counting easier.

Did you know?

For these children in Colombia in South America, the quickest way to get to school is by zip wire!

a   How many children in Zara's class think that children can walk or cycle safely to school? ....

b   How many of their classmates don't think that cars are a safe way to travel to school? ....

c   How many of their classmates are not sure if the amount of exhaust fumes on their school run too high? ....

What questions can we ask in our survey?

1   You are going to do a survey similar to the one Zara and her group did. You can make up your own questions, but you may like to find out:

-   how your classmates travel to school and what they think about it
-   if they would prefer to come to school in a different way
-   if they think their journey affects other people and the environment.

Talk to your partner about six questions you can ask. Try to think of ones that are relevant to your school. Choose questions that children can answer 'yes', 'no' or 'I'm not sure' to.

environment

relevant

Copy the table below and write your questions.

Questions about our journey to school	Yes	No	I'm not sure

2 Carry out your survey. Record children's answers in the table by putting a tally mark in the correct column for 'yes', 'no' or 'I'm not sure'.

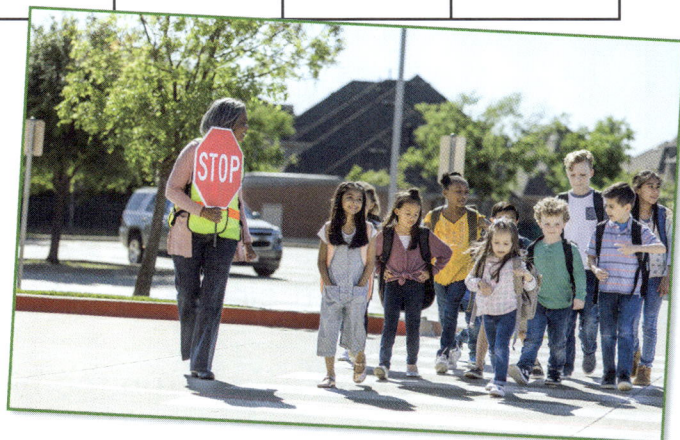

3 Then complete these sentences:

We asked .... children.

One thing my survey shows is that ....

....

More than half the class think that ....

....

Only a few children say that ....

....

What did we all find out?

Discuss the information you have found out with **your group**.
Talk about how you and your classmates feel **about the way**
you all travel to and from school.

Write three interesting things that you and your **classmates**
talked about:

1　...

2　...

3　...

〉 1.3　Are some ways of travelling to school better than others?

Learning goals		
Our learning goals	**I think**	**My teacher thinks**
I can talk about a source and what it says about the issue.	★ ☺ 😐	★ ☺ 😐 ....
I can give reasons for my opinion about an issue.	★ ☺ 😐	★ ☺ 😐 ....

Where can we find more information about sustainable journeys?

sustainable

local

pollution

1   Zara's neighbour has moved to another area. He has sent her a photograph. It shows him going to school by scooter. On the back of the photograph, he has written a note.

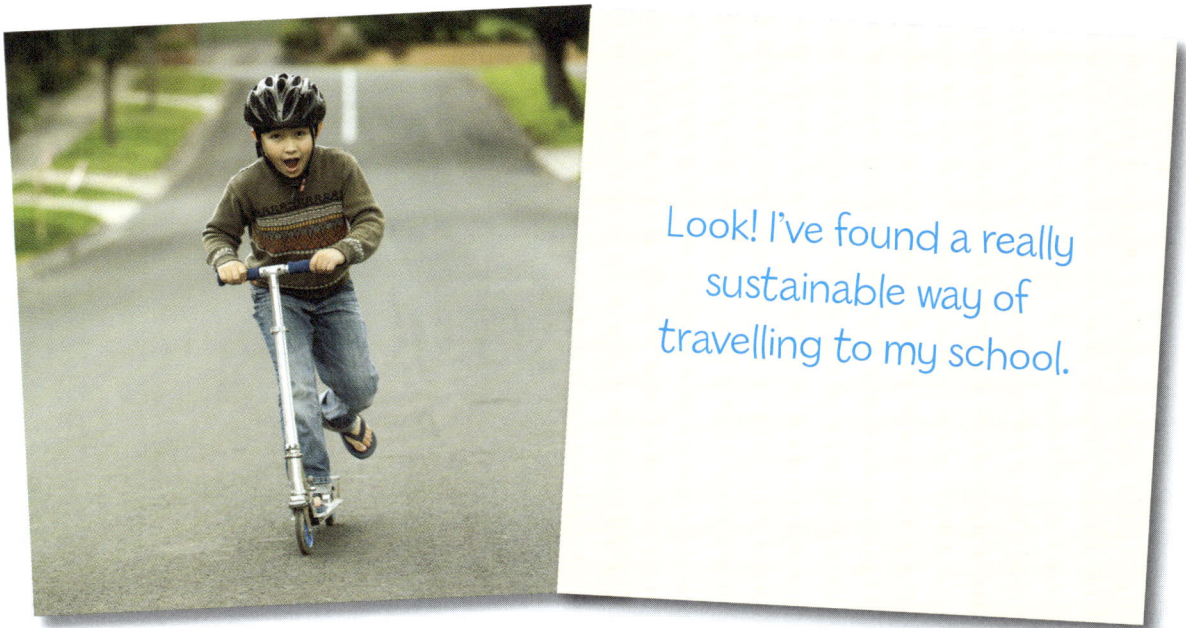

Look! I've found a really sustainable way of travelling to my school.

Zara found out that 'sustainable' means 'causing little or no damage to the environment'.

What do you think is good or not so good about going to school by scooter?

2   Zara and Arun's group decide to find out more about different ways of travelling to their school. They want to know if some are more sustainable than others.

They begin by looking for good sources of information about their local area, Westside. Talk to your partner about these sources and answer the questions.

A social media report

Plan to build more bike lanes too expensive, says president of Erlandia

A leaflet

A travel plan for Westside schools

Walk, cycle, scoot or take the bus to school in Westside

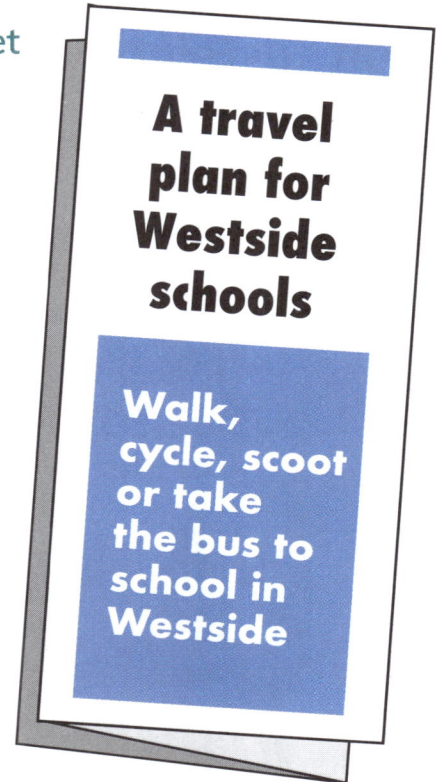

A newspaper article

Westside Observer
Local news for local people

Exhaust fumes survey on busy Westside street

See page 8 for details

a   Which source will give the group information about traffic pollution

in the local area? ....

b   Which source will give them information about sustainable ways

of travelling to school? ....

c   Do you think more bike lanes should be built in Erlandia?
Circle your answer

because   so that   necessary

Yes   No

Explain your answer ....

....

Can sustainable school journeys help the environment?

1 Read the school travel plan leaflet. It describes how sustainable school journeys can **improve** things for people and the environment. After you've read the leaflet you can answer the question.

improve

MAKING TRAVEL PLANS FOR WESTSIDE SCHOOLS

A School Travel Plan describes how to cut down on journeys made by car and develop safer, healthier ways of travelling to and from school.

A Travel Plan can help with issues such as:

- traffic jams at the beginning and end of the school day

- children's health, well-being and activity levels

- keeping roads safe at busy times

- traffic fumes, air quality and climate change.

WHY DO YOU NEED A SCHOOL TRAVEL PLAN?

Active travel means modes of transport like walking or cycling. Children could do this for all or part of their journey. Active travel benefits the school, local community and the wider area by reducing the amount of traffic on the roads.

For children
- Active travel improves health and fitness levels.
- Develops children's safety skills on roads.
- Helps children to concentrate better at school.

For the school
- Improves safety on roads near the school.
- Cuts down on the amount of traffic near the school.
- Develops safer routes near the school.

For families
- Makes less stress.
- Cuts down on time spent driving to school on busy roads.
- Provides time to talk to each other while walking to school.

For the local community
- Cuts down on amounts of air pollution and noise.
- Makes the area's roads less busy.
- Improves road safety for the whole area.
- Develops safer routes for everyone.

Read the sentences. Who will benefit from each change? Write **children, school, families** or **local community** by each statement.

a   Less traffic near school ....

b   Active travel makes you fitter and healthier ....

c   Less time spent driving on busy roads ....

d   Less air and noise pollution ....

e   Active travel helps you concentrate better in class ....

f   Better walking routes ....

g   More time for talking ....

h   Safer roads around school ....

2   Zara has started a discussion about sustainable school journeys. Listen to the opinions shared by Zara, Arun, Sofia and Marcus. Tick the opinion that is most similar to your opinion. ✓

Share your ideas with the other children in your group.

3   After the discussion, do you still think the same way?
     Write the character whose opinion you agree with most now.
     You can change your mind, but you don't have to.

   I now agree with ....'s opinion the most.

   This is because ....

   ....

4   If you want to travel to school more sustainably, what do you
     think you could do to make it possible?

Did you know?

Some schools have **W**alk **O**n **W**ednesdays – **WOW**! Every
Wednesday, children try to make a sustainable journey to school.
They can:

- cycle
- scoot
- use **public transport**
- walk the whole way
- walk some of the way.

public transport

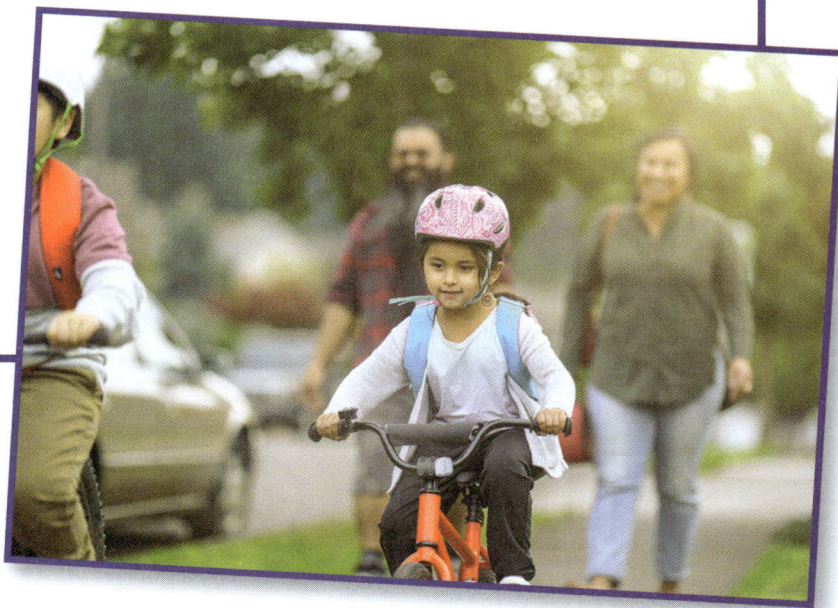

> 1.4 How can my group tell people about sustainable travel?

Learning goals		
Our learning goals	**I think**	**My teacher thinks**
I can help the group decide what tasks each group member will do.	★ ☺ 😐	★ ☺ 😐 ....
I can work well with other group members to achieve our group's goal.	★ ☺ 😐	★ ☺ 😐 ....

How can we work together in my group?

You are going to prepare a presentation with your group. Your presentation will tell people what you have found out about sustainable ways of travelling.

You may be able to do your presentation by showing slides on a whiteboard or by making posters. Talk to your teacher about the best way to do it.

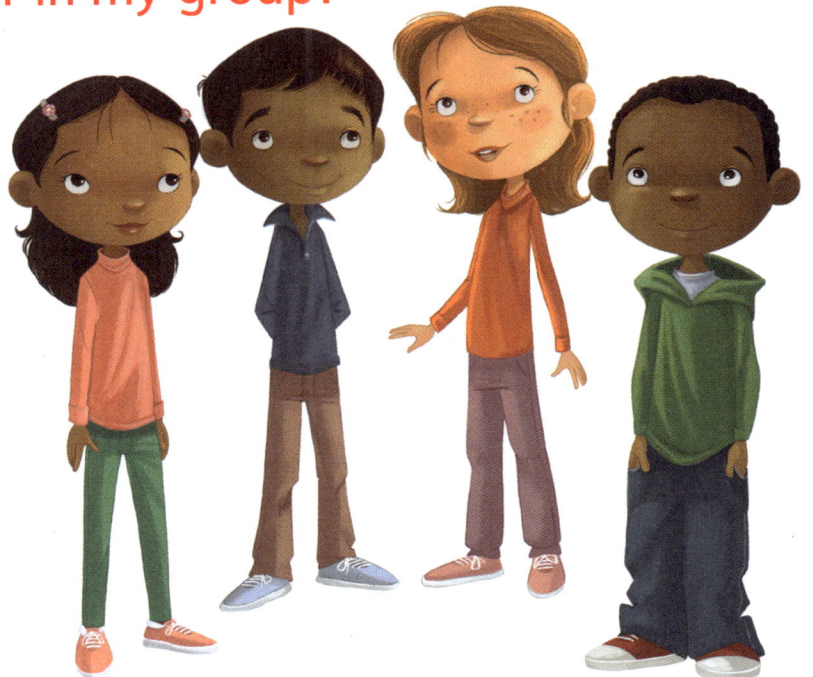

1   With your group, decide how you will work together.
    Write three points about good teamwork that you
    all agree on:

Good teamwork happens when:

....

....

....

Share your ideas with the rest of the class.

2   Sofia and Marcus have had a discussion in their group
    about their presentation. They have made a plan.

Our group's presentation about sustainable school journeys

(by Arun, Marcus, Sofia, Zara)

Who?

Part 1   Say what our presentation is about.   Everybody

Part 2   Explain the problem.

Part 3   Report what you found out about the issue.

Part 4   Describe a sustainable travel plan.

Part 5   Next steps – can we try a Sustainable Travel Day?

The group decide who will be responsible for each part of the presentation. They agree that they will do Part 1 together then they will each take one of the other parts.

Read what each person says they will do.
Then write the number of the part from their plan.

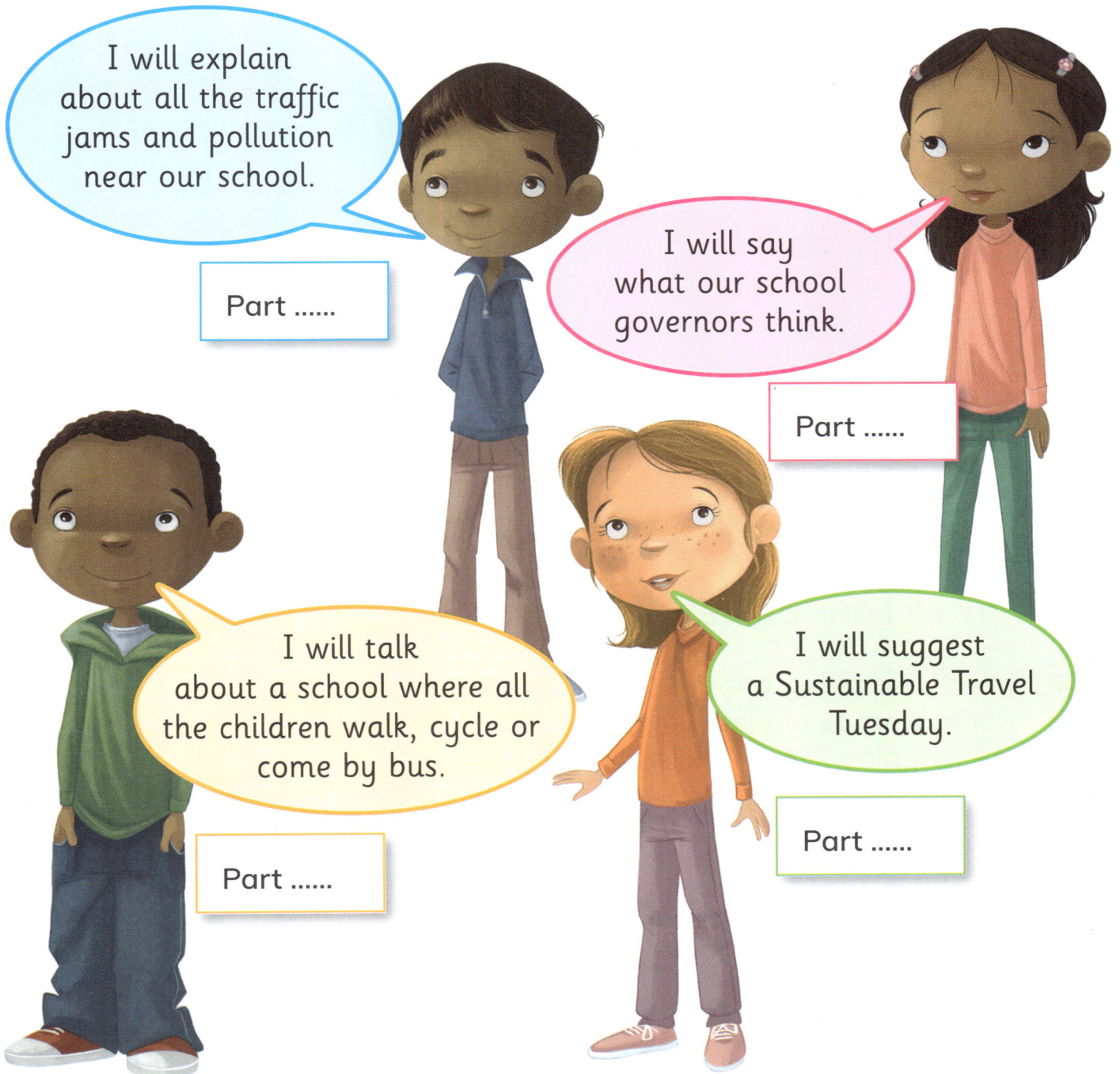

I will explain about all the traffic jams and pollution near our school.

Part ......

I will say what our school governors think.

Part ......

I will talk about a school where all the children walk, cycle or come by bus.

Part ......

I will suggest a Sustainable Travel Tuesday.

Part ......

3   Now make a plan with your own group. Copy the plan below in your notebook. Add as many parts as you need.

Talk about:

- the number of parts you need
- what each part will be about
- who will be responsible for each part.

Our group's presentation about sustainable school journeys

(by ...., ..., ..., ...)

		Who?
Part 1	Say what our presentation is about.	....
Part 2	....	....
Part 3	....	....
Part 4	....	....
Part 5	....	....

What will our presentation look like?

1   With your group, talk about what to put into your presentation. The checklist will help you.

You can make notes and tick the boxes to help you remember what you decide.

Things to think about for our presentation

• Who will we ask and how will we get information from them?

....

• How can we find out about schools with sustainable travel plans?

....

• How could we plan a Sustainable Travel Day for our school?

....

Things we could include for people to look at

Pictures showing traffic near our school.   ☐

A map showing our school and the local area.   ☐

Pictures, maps or information about local cycling and walking routes.   ☐

Pictures showing children travelling in a sustainable way.   ☐

My group's idea:

....   ☐

2 Look back at the plan your group made for your presentation.
Which part are you responsible for?

I am responsible for ....

Talk with your group about what each of you will do. Then fill in the information about your part of the presentation.

Top tip

Try making a to-do list to help you think about and record what information and images you need.

I will talk about	Information sources I will use	Slides or pictures I will include (like images and maps)

3   You are now ready to make your presentation!
Prepare your slides or your posters.

> **Top tip**
>
> Choose colours and fonts that will be eye-catching but easy
> to read. In your group, decide on a 'house style' by agreeing
> on the same colours and fonts. A 'house style' means that all
> your slides or all your posters should look as though they belong
> together. For example you could use 'bubble writing' for all
> headings and use the same colour for each one.

〉 1.5   How can we make our presentation as good as possible?

Learning goals

Our learning goals	I think	My teacher thinks
I can talk to an audience about an issue.	★ ☺ ☺	★ ☺ ☺ ....
I can ask questions in a discussion.	★ ☺ ☺	★ ☺ ☺ ....

How will we show our presentation to the class?

1 Zara and Arun's group have been talking about how to make their presentation really good. They have started to make some notes. Finish the sentences for them.

- It is important to face our audience because

  ....

- It is important to speak clearly so that

  ....

2 Zara and Arun's group have also written a checklist of things to discuss before they do their presentation in front of other people. Use their checklist with your own group. Tick each thing after you have discussed it.

☐ Make sure we all know in what order we will speak.

☐ Make sure we know what we need to say in our part.

☐ Decide what we need to point to when we are talking.

☐ Decide how we will let the next person know when it is their turn to speak.

3 Practise your presentation with your group.
   Make any last-minute changes you feel you need to.

4 You are now ready to show your presentation to your class.

> **Top tip**
>
> Smile and look at your audience! Don't read too much from your notes.

5 Watch other groups' presentations. As you watch, try to think of:

One thing you liked

It was really interesting when you said . . .

Can you explain . . . ?

One question

One thing they could improve

I think it would be even better if . . .

Can we improve our presentations?

Marcus and Sofia have finished their presentation.
They are discussing the things that they should change.

> Some children couldn't read the yellow writing on our slide.

> We should use a darker colour instead. It would be easier to read.

Talk with your group. What worked well in your presentation?
What could you improve? Write your ideas here.

The best thing about our presentation was ....

....

Our presentation could be even better if ....

....

› 1.6 What have we learned during this project?

Learning goals		
Our learning goals	**I think**	**My teacher thinks**
I can talk about something I have learned during the project.	★ ☺ 😐	★ ☺ 😐 ....
I can describe an activity that helped me learn something.	★ ☺ 😐	★ ☺ 😐 ....
I can say how my ideas have changed during the project.	★ ☺ 😐	★ ☺ 😐 ....

What have we found out about sustainable travel?

Zara, Arun, Marcus and Sofia are **reflecting** on the work they have done in their project. They are writing their reflections.

reflect

1 Zara has learned a lot of new things about travelling to school.

> Something I have learned that I didn't know before
>
> Exhaust fumes are bad for our health.
> Before, I just thought they smelled horrible.

Think about something you have found out in this project that you didn't know before.

> Something I have learned that I didn't know before
>
> _____
>
> _____

2 Marcus remembers an activity that helped him learn something useful.

> Something I learned that helped me
>
> I learned how to ask questions that you can only answer 'yes' or 'no' to. This helped me to make a survey about journeys to school.

Think about an activity that helped you learn something useful. What did you learn? How did it help you?

> Something I learned that helped me
>
> _____
>
> _____

3   Sofia and Arun have thought about sustainable travel. They have written what they thought at the beginning of the project and what they think now.

What was your opinion at the start of this project? What is your opinion now?

My opinion about sustainable travel

At the beginning, I thought that how I travelled to school was not important. Now I think that coming to school in a sustainable way could really make my town better.

– Arun

My opinion about sustainable travel

At the beginning, I didn't know anything about sustainable travel. Finding out about it was interesting but I still think cars are a good way of getting around.

– Sofia

My opinion about sustainable travel

_____

_____

_____

_____

_____

_____

How did we help each other in our group?

Arun is thinking about how the members of his group helped each other during their project.

> Sofia showed me how to **crop** digital photographs for my part of our presentation. I helped Zara with spellings.

1   Work with your group. Think about all the activities you have completed together. Talk about the things you did to help each other, then answer the questions.

crop

a   What helpful thing did each person in the group do for your presentation?

Name	How they helped
....	....
....	....
....	....
....	....
....	....

b   How well did the group work together?   ★   ☺   😐

c   Do you think your group was successful in your task
     to tell other children about sustainable transport?   ★   ☺   😐

Explain your reason: ....

2   Ask your group to help you complete this sentence.

My group thought it was helpful when I ....

3   Complete this sentence by yourself.

My group helped me to ....

What can we tell each other about what we have learned?

Talk with a partner from your group.

Ask them to look at these statements
and (circle) the best symbol for you.

How well does your partner think that you:

Listened to others in the group?   ★   ☺   😐

Made some helpful suggestions?   ★   ☺   😐

Helped the group to agree?   ★   ☺   😐

What have we learned?

Look back over your learning goals in this project. Finish these sentences.

In this project I learned how to ....

Something I did well on this project was ....

Next time I want to be able to ....

2 Can we help children to eat well?

PUMPKIN

CAPSICUM

TURNIP

BRINJAL

CARROT

EAT 5 A DAY

NOODLES FANTASTIC NEW FLAVOUR!

Marcus

TOMATO

WATERMELON

POTATO

CABBAGE

BUY 2 CAKES GET 1 FREE

Sofia

OUR LOWEST PRICE

> 2.1 What kinds of foods and drinks do we have?

Learning goals		
Our learning goals	**I think**	**My teacher thinks**
I can describe what other people think about an issue.	★ ☺ ☺	★ ☺ ☺ ....
I can think of something I could do to make a difference to other people.	★ ☺ ☺	★ ☺ ☺ ....

What types of foods do we like to eat?

1   a   These are lots of words that we can use to talk about food or drink.

Look at these words and answer the questions with a partner

Do we usually use the words to describe foods, or drinks or both?
Write **foods**, **drinks** or **foods and drinks** next to each word.

sweet ....foods and drinks.......

spicy ....

junk ....

crunchy ....

healthy ....

fizzy ....

take-away ....

b   Do you like each of these kinds of foods and drinks?
Can you say why or why not?

2 Two people are thinking about the types of foods they like or don't like eating.

It's hard to find things all my family like. I love chicken biryani but my children say it's too spicy.

Oh no, not soup again. I wish I could have something with crunchy vegetables in it.

What types of foods do **you** like to eat?

junk food

3 Read four people's opinions about food. Draw a line to match each person to their opinion about food. Then draw a ☺ if they like it or a ☹ if they don't.

1

Adam

2

Nisha

3

Kojo

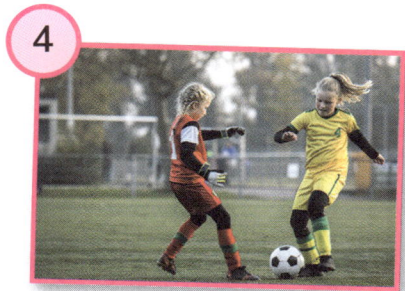

4

Ana and Elana

a My dad makes me a packed lunch to take to school. He always puts crunchy carrot sticks in because I can eat them fast then go and play!

b We like to eat foods that give us lots of energy so we can keep moving when we do sport. Our Mum says 'pasta makes you go fasta!' Luckily, we both love it!

c I usually have take-away food for lunch. My favourite is burger and chips. I know eating a lot of junk food is not very healthy, but I don't have much time when I'm working.

d I make laddu when my grandchildren come to visit. They are too sweet for me, but my grandchildren love them. Maybe I should try serving fresh mango instead – it would be better for their teeth!

4 Now answer the questions:

a Who thinks fresh fruit is more healthy than sweets? ....

b Who eats a lot of junk food? ....

c Which food is useful if you do a lot of sport? ....

d Which two people choose food they can eat quickly?

....

e Why do different people choose different foods? Explain your ideas.

....

....

prefer   convenient   favourite

f Do you think that some foods are more **nutritious** than others? (Circle) your answer.

nutritious

Yes   No

Why do you think this? Choose useful sentence parts from the box to help you explain your answer:

Some foods help us because they..

....

Some foods are not so good for our body because they ....

....

have a lot of sugar in them   give us energy

help us grow   keep our bodies working properly

have a lot of salt in them

What do we have to drink?

1   What do you like to drink?
Work with a partner and write your ideas in your diagrams.

- If you like a kind of drink and your partner doesn't, write it in your yellow shape.

- If your partner likes a kind of drink and you don't, write it in your blue shape.

- If you both like the same drink, write it in the middle green part.

hydrated

Did you know?

Did you know that around 70 percent of the human body is water? Water keeps our brains, bones, heart and teeth healthy, and it makes them work well. If we drink enough water, we can say that we are 'well hydrated'. When we are well hydrated, we feel happier and we can concentrate for longer.

Drinks I like   Drinks my partner likes

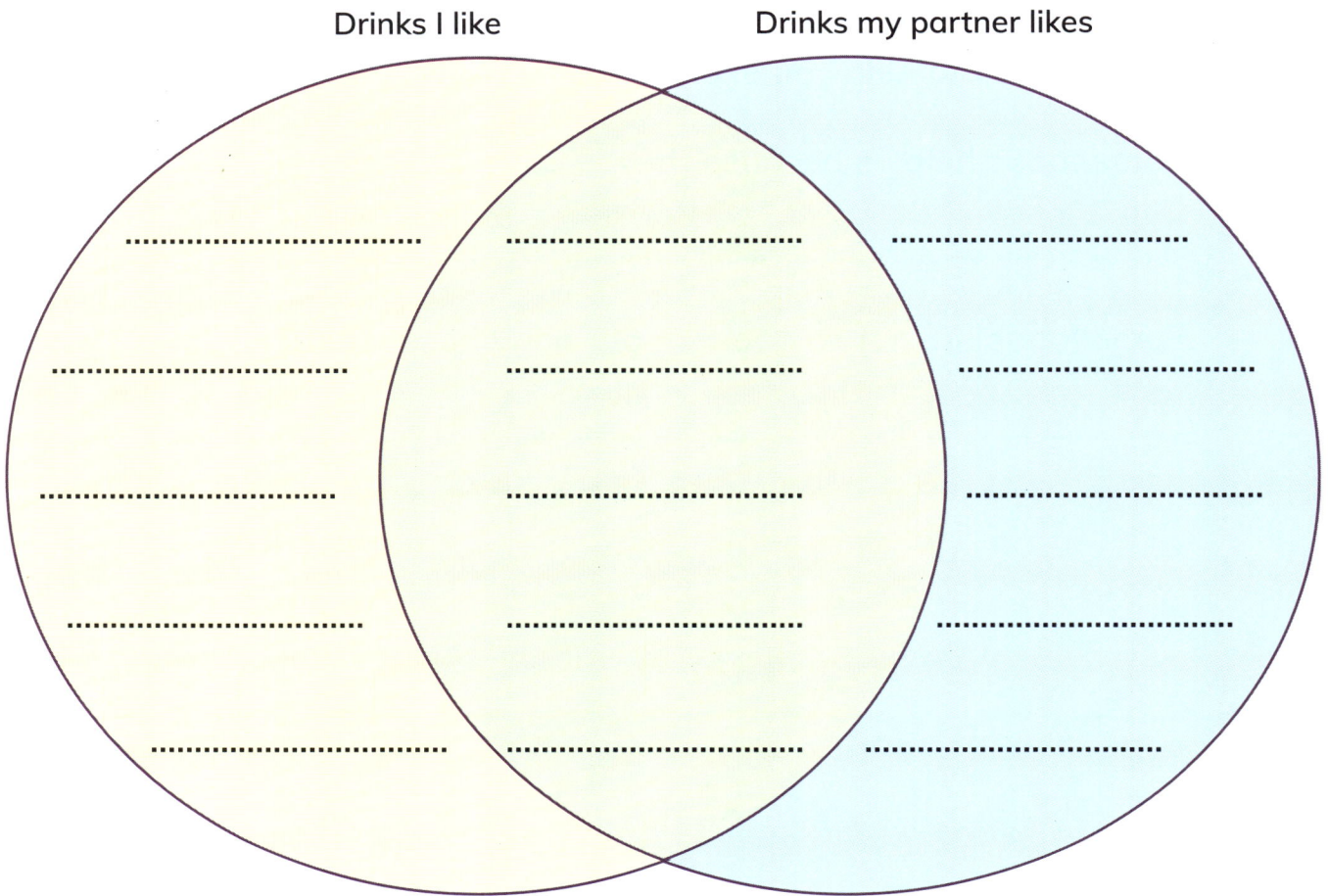

Look at your completed diagram. Do you and your partner like mainly the same drinks or mainly different drinks?

2   Does it matter what kind of drinks we have? Why? Tell your partner.
   Circle the drink you think we should drink the most:

   fruit juice   fizzy drinks   water

Explain your answer: ....

....

How could you find out which type of drink is most healthy?

....

3 Lots of people like fizzy drinks.
   Talk to your partner about why that could be. Write two reasons here:
   Younger children often like fizzy drinks

   because ....

   and ....

4 Imagine you are trying to persuade younger children to drink more water.
   Read these ideas together and tick (✓)the ones you think might work:

role model

1 Be a **role model**. Show young children that you enjoy drinking water.

2 Give them a special cup – for example, with a picture of their favourite cartoon character on.

3 Tell adults to stop buying fizzy drinks. If they don't buy them, children can't drink them!

4 Decorate their water bottle with stickers (flowers, cars, dinosaurs, sports stars, etc.).

5 Try adding a piece of fresh fruit or cucumber to water to give it a nice taste.

Which idea sounds best? Write the number in the box:

Explain your answer:

I think the best idea is to ....

....

....

> 2.2 Which kinds of food and drink are better for us?

Learning goals		
Our learning goals	**I think**	**My teacher thinks**
I can find information and the answers to questions in a source.	★ ☺ ☺	★ ☺ ☺ ....
I can organise and record information in a table.	★ ☺ ☺	★ ☺ ☺ ....

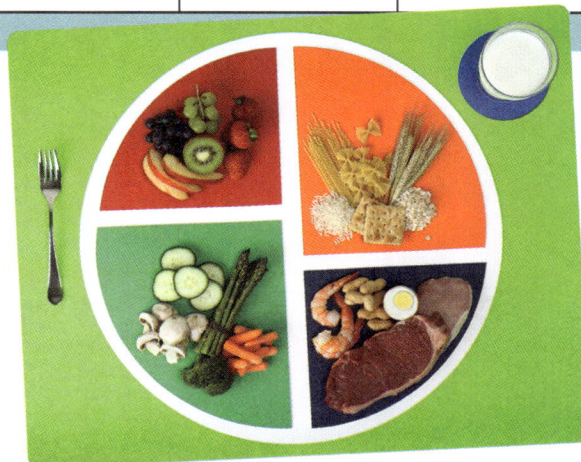

How can we find out more about different types of food and drink?

Arun, Marcus and their group want to find out what foods they should eat and how much of each kind of food.

> My dad says we should eat five portions of fruit and vegetables every day.

> My mum says that, too. What other foods do we need to eat to stay healthy?

They find a diagram of a food pyramid.

With your partner, discuss the answers to the questions about the food pyramid.

a What type of food can you see in each level of the pyramid (from 1 to 4)?

b What do you think the food pyramid shows us?

food group

fat

vitamins and minerals

carbohydrate

protein

How much we should eat of different types of food.

OR

Which types of food children like the most.

Explain your answer.

Why is food divided into different groups?

Food can be divided into different food groups. Each group contains the nutritious foods that give us energy, keep our bodies working properly, help us grow and heal.

1 Look at the food groups in the table. Fill in the missing sections.

Food group	Examples of foods in this group	Used by the body for	Which level in the food pyramid has the most?
Fats	Cooking oil, ghee, butter	Energy	1
Vitamins and minerals		Keep our bodies working properly	3
Carbohydrates	Bread, pasta, noodles, rice	Energy	

Food group	Examples of foods in this group	Used by the body for	Which level in the food pyramid has the most?
Proteins		Growth and repair	

2   Now answer these questions using the table and the pyramid:

a   Protein is needed for: ....

Why do you think this is especially important for children?

....

b   How do fresh fruit and vegetables help us stay healthy?

....

....

c   Which should we eat more of: fats or carbohydrates?

Explain your answer ....

....

....

Did you know?

Our bodies also need water to stay healthy.
We should try to drink between six and eight
glasses of water every day.

What is a healthy lunch for children?

Here are some photographs of different lunches. Talk to your classmates about the types and amounts of food in the lunches. Are they good lunches for a child? How could you make them healthier?

> 2.3 What do young children know about types of foods and drinks?

Learning goals		
Our learning goals	**I think**	**My teacher thinks**
I can talk about information sources and what their authors might think.	★ ☺ ☺	★ ☺ ☺ ....
I can give reasons for my opinion about an issue.	★ ☺ ☺	★ ☺ ☺ ....

What can sources tell us about healthy eating?

1   Sofia's teacher has been helping Sofia's class to talk online to children in another school. The school is far away, in another country. Sofia's class asked the children in the other school how they encourage younger children to eat healthy foods at their school. Read the email that the other school sent.

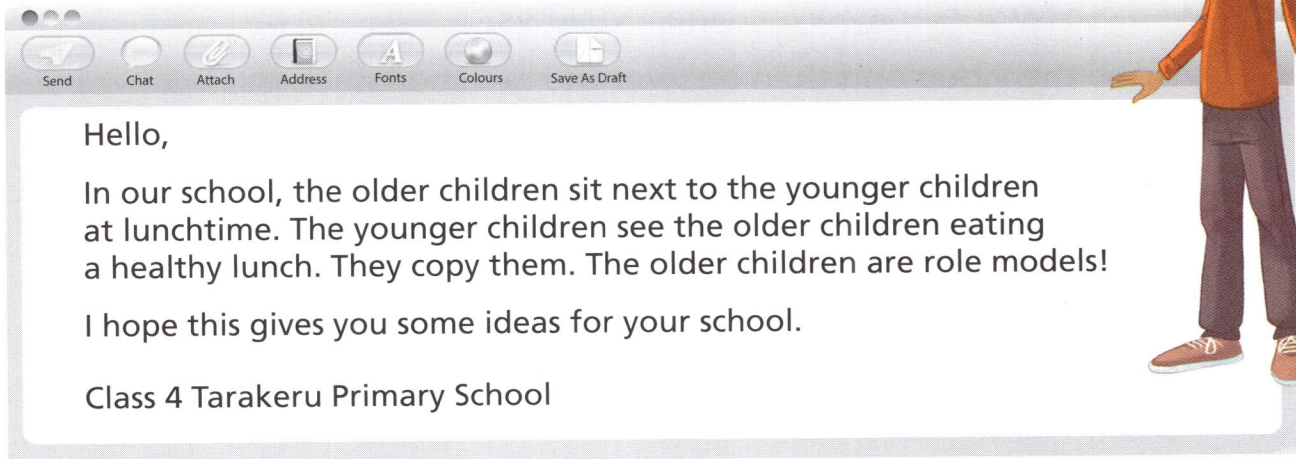

Send	Chat	Attach	Address	Fonts	Colours	Save As Draft

Hello,

In our school, the older children sit next to the younger children at lunchtime. The younger children see the older children eating a healthy lunch. They copy them. The older children are role models!

I hope this gives you some ideas for your school.

Class 4 Tarakeru Primary School

Sofia's group think that having older children to act as role models is a good idea. Talk to your partner about what happens at lunchtime or break time in your school:

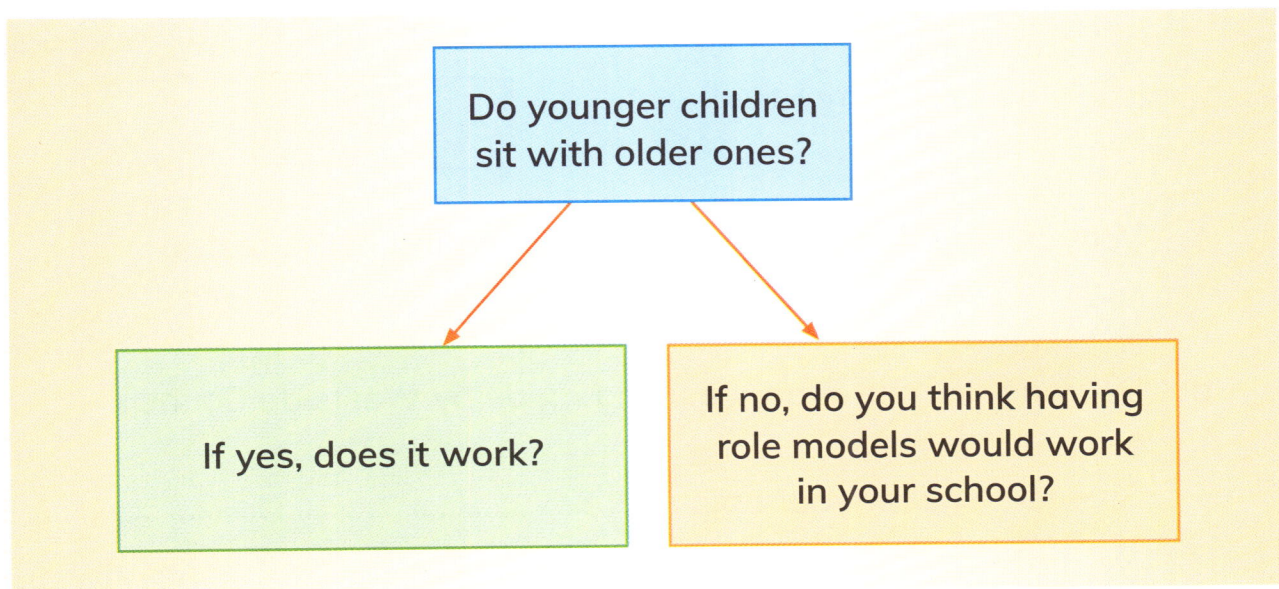

Do younger children sit with older ones?

If yes, does it work?

If no, do you think having role models would work in your school?

2 Sofia's group decide to find out more about what young children know and feel about different foods. They also want to know what affects the way that young children feel about food.

They look at some different sources.

They start with a report on the news website for their city, Westside TV News.

Watch the video and then answer the questions:

a What types of food are Westside schools and street stalls near them not allowed to sell any more?

....

b Does the stallholder think this is a good idea? Why or why not?

Explain your answer ....

c (Circle) the person who says this:

> It's so relaxing to eat here and my little girl loves getting a free toy!

a stall holder

a scientist

a customer

Why do you think this person enjoys eating in the restaurant?

....

d Do you think the changes being made by Westside Council are a good idea?

Give reasons for your opinion. ....

....

3   Next, Sofia's group find an information leaflet.

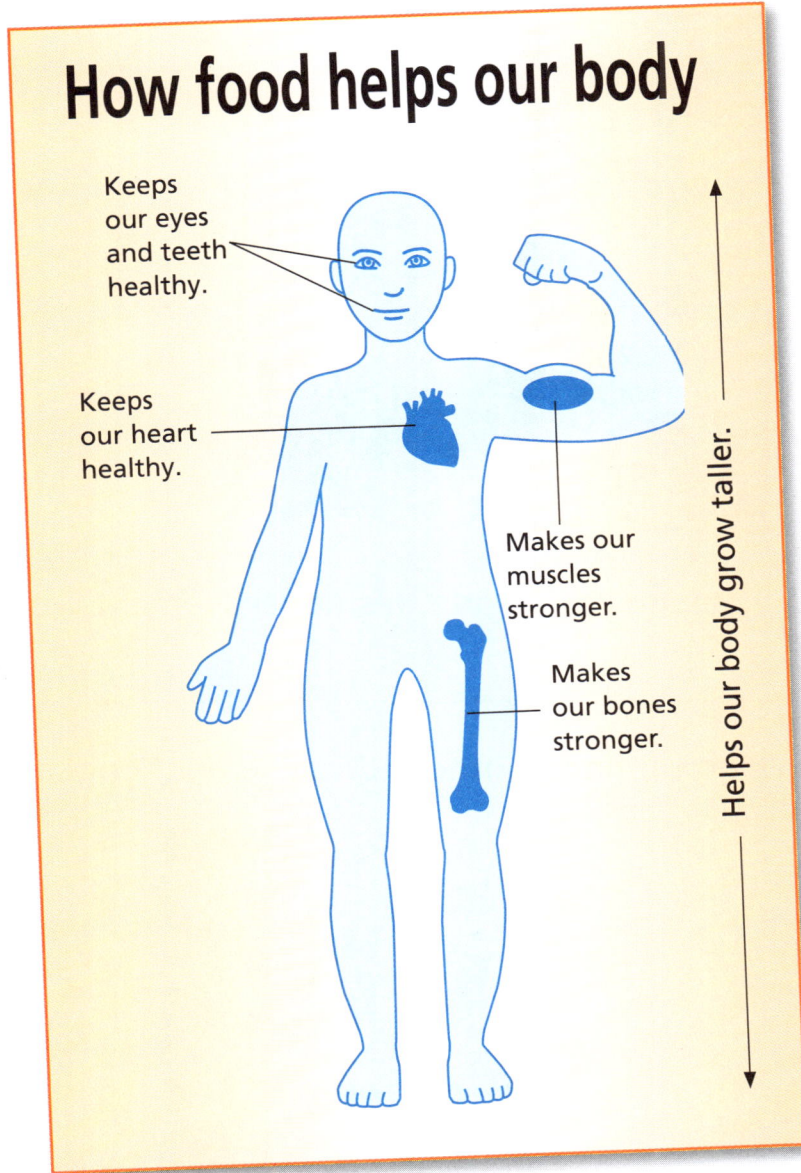

How food helps our body

Keeps our eyes and teeth healthy.

Keeps our heart healthy.

Makes our muscles stronger.

Makes our bones stronger.

Helps our body grow taller.

Do you think the person who made this information leaflet thinks healthy eating is important for children?

Explain how you can tell. ....

....

4   Then Sofia's group find an advertisement in a restaurant.

How does the person who made this advertisement want people to feel?

....

5   Finally, Sofia's group find another advertisement online.

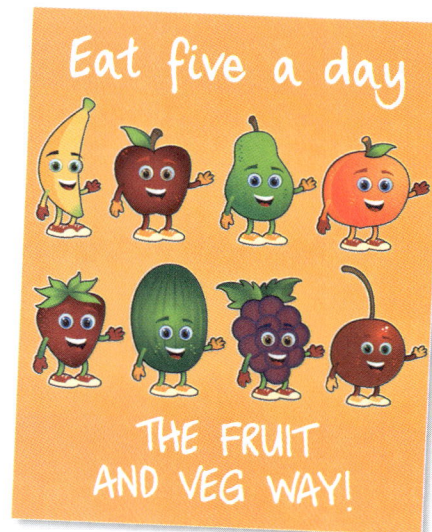

What is the **purpose** of this poster?
Explain how you can tell.

purpose

....

How can we encourage young children to make healthy choices?

1   Zara's group want to help younger children understand how to choose healthy food. They think it would be a good idea to make a book.

They make a list of things they want to find out about information books for younger children:

Information books for young children

Text
- Are the sentences short?
- Do the books use words that young children will understand?

Pictures
- Do the books have colourful pictures or photos?

Special features for young children
- Are there any fun characters who explain things?

Look at three information books for younger children.

In your group, copy this table and make notes about the three books. Use Zara's group's checklist.

Name of book	Text	Pictures	Special features for young children
1			
2			
3			

2   You are going to work with your group to make an information book for younger children. It will be about healthy foods and drinks.

What do you think it should look like?

- Give an example of an **important fact** about healthy eating to put in your book.

....

- Suggest a picture or photo to put in your book.

....

- Suggest a **fun feature** that would have special appeal for younger children.

....

> **Top tip**
>
> Think about the books you have looked at – colourful headings, patterns, decorations and exciting pictures of characters will all appeal to younger children.

3   Think about younger children in school or in your family.
Do they know which foods and drinks are healthy?
(Circle) your answer.   Yes   No

How can you tell? ....

> **Did you know?**
>
> Bananas are a good source of the minerals we need to keep our heart healthy. Banana skin can help stop the itching when a mosquito bites you. Bananas also float in water!

> 2.4 How can we work together to complete an information book for young children?

Learning goals		
Our learning goals	**I think**	**My teacher thinks**
I can help my group decide what tasks each group member will do.	★ ☺ ☺	★ ☺ ☺ ....
I can work well with my group to achieve our group's goal.	★ ☺ ☺	★ ☺ ☺ ....

How can we work together in our group?

1 Zara and Arun went to their school canteen to do some research while the youngest children were eating their lunch. They wanted to find out what types of food the children were choosing.

Listen to Zara and Arun telling their group about their visit.

a What did Zara and Arun want to find out?

b What problems did they find out about?

c What do Zara and Arun need to do next?

2   Before Arun's group start making their information book, they need to make sure they know what the parts of the book are called.

With a partner, label the information book using the words from the box.

author   picture   title   blurb

Front cover

a

Fun Facts on Food

Selma Rice

b

Back cover

c

Learn all about how to stay healthy with this fun-filled book of amazing food facts.

d

3 Arun and his group have had a discussion together about their information book. Look at the plan they have made.

Our group's information book about a healthy eating plan for younger children

by Arun, Zara, Sofia, Marcus

Front and back cover We need to choose a title and picture

Part 1   Explain what the book will say

Part 2   Explain why a healthy eating plan is important for children

Part 3   Explain what amounts of different foods we need to eat

Part 3   Explain what happens at lunchtime in our canteen

The group decide who will be responsible for each part of the book. They agree that they will all make the covers together and they will each take one of the other parts.

Read what each person says they will do.
Then write the number of the part from their plan.

I'll make a simple food pyramid diagram and explain what it shows.

Part ......

I'll give information about our menus and where you can sit to eat.

Part ......

I'll say what the book is about and make it sound exciting.

Part ......

I'll say how our body uses different foods.

Part ......

4 Now have a discussion with your group. Make a plan like the one below.

Talk about:

- How many pages you need for each part.

- What you will put on each page.

- Who will be responsible for each part of the book. Make sure everybody knows what they are going to do!

Parts of our book	Pictures	Our ideas for this part of the book	Who is responsible?
Front cover With title and authors			
Part 1 Say what young children need to know to eat healthily			
Part 2 Why a healthy diet is important			
Part 3 Healthy eating pyramid			
Part 4 Our school canteen			
Back cover With blurb			

Top tips

- Think of an exciting title for your book.
- Think about lunchtimes in your school – can you get photographs or menus?
- Listen to each other's ideas!

Did you know?

A berry is a type of fruit with seeds on the inside. But did you know that a strawberry has 200 seeds on the outside, so actually it's <u>not</u> a berry? On the other hand, a pomegranate has 1000 seeds inside – so it is a berry!

What will our information book look like?

1 You are ready to start making your information book with your group.

Are you going to write your pages by hand or work with a computer and print them out? Talk to your teacher about this.

blurb

With your group, use this checklist to help you remember everything.

Things to think about when we make our information book

Remember who is responsible for each part. ☐

Check what you have found out about healthy foods and drinks. ☐

Remember what you have found out about books for younger children. ☐

2 Talk with your group about what each page will look like. Think about: characters, colours for paper and text, and any special features you want to add.

Then fill in the information about your section of the book.

Part of the book I am responsible for	What it will look like	Our ideas for this part of the book

3 Follow these stages to make your information book.

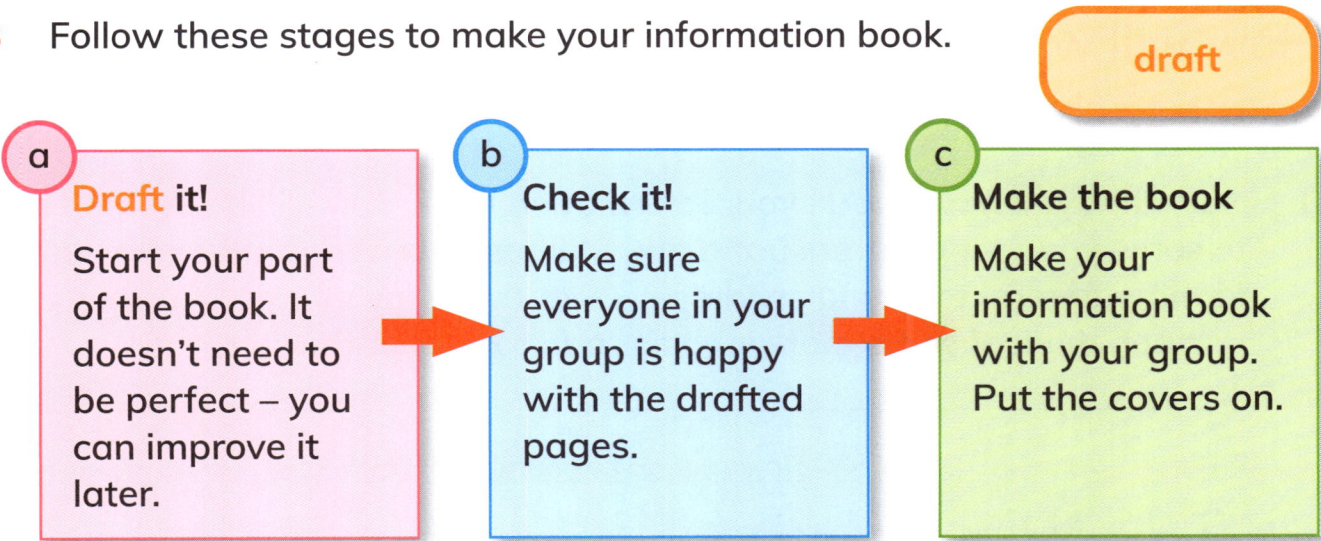

draft

a **Draft it!**
Start your part of the book. It doesn't need to be perfect – you can improve it later.

b **Check it!**
Make sure everyone in your group is happy with the drafted pages.

c **Make the book**
Make your information book with your group. Put the covers on.

❯ 2.5 Can our information book tell younger children about healthy eating?

Learning goals		
Our learning goals	**I think**	**My teacher thinks**
I can talk about an issue clearly.	★ ☺ 😐	★ ☺ 😐 ....
I can respond to what someone says in a class discussion by asking them a question.	★ ☺ 😐	★ ☺ 😐 ....

How will we share our information book with younger children?

1 Now that you have made your information book, you will be reading it to some younger children. Sofia and Marcus have thought of some ideas for how to read to young children so that they stay interested. With your partner, think of some more ideas to add to the list they started.

<u>How to read to younger children</u>

- Sit somewhere comfortable.
- Speak clearly and not too quickly.
- Decide what you need to point to or talk about on each page.
- ....
- ....
- ....

2 Talk about your ideas with the rest of your group. Check that you all agree on how you will share your book, and think about how you would like your audience to react!

3   Before you read your book with the younger children, you are going to practise sharing it with some children in your class.

Work with another group. Take turns to read your book to each other. After each book, discuss what worked well and what could be even better. Remember to **always** start by giving positive feedback.

Use this checklist as you listen to the other group reading their book.

Did they explain everything clearly?	Yes	No
Did they point to the right part of the page?	Yes	No
Did they make it fun?	Yes	No

What did you enjoy most about the reading?

....

Is there something that would make their reading even better?

....

Can we improve our reading?

Arun and Zara reflect on how it went when they practised sharing their book with another group.

I think we need to make our message about choosing healthy foods and drinks clearer.

Reading a book aloud is like acting. You have to pretend to be the characters and keep your audience's attention.

1   Talk with your group about what went well in your reading practice and what you could do better next time. Record your ideas here:

The best thing about our group's reading practice was:

....

The thing that the other group most enjoyed was:

....

Our reading would be even better if:

....

2   Decide with your group what last-minute changes you want to make.

3   Share your book with some younger children.

Did our audience enjoy our reading?

1   After all the groups in your class have shared their book with younger children, have a class discussion. Talk about these questions. Have all the children in your class had a similar experience? Do they all agree?

2   How did your audience react when you shared your book with them? Did they:

- Listen carefully?
- Ask questions?
- Answer your questions?
- Laugh and smile?
- Sit still?

Which parts went well?

....

What would you do differently if you were
going to read your book to younger children again?

....

....

Do you think your audience knows more about healthy
eating now that you have shared your book with them?

....

> 2.6 What have we learned during this project?

Learning goals		
Our learning goals	**I think**	**My teacher thinks**
I can talk about how working as a team helped us to achieve our goal.	★ ☺ ☺	★ ☺ ☺ ....
I can describe an activity that helped me learn something.	★ ☺ ☺	★ ☺ ☺ ....

What have we found out during this project?

Sofia and Marcus are reflecting on what they have learned in their project about healthy foods and drinks. They remember what they used to think about going shopping for their family's groceries, what they have learned during the project and how they feel now:

I've told my family we need to make healthier choices.

I still love fizzy drinks but I'll try to drink them less often.

1   Think about what you have learned during the project that you didn't know before.

Something I have learned about food and drink that I didn't know before

....

....

Something I have learned about books and reading for young children

....

....

2 How have your ideas changed since the beginning of the project?

How my ideas have changed

At the beginning ....

....

Now ....

....

3 Think about something you learned from an activity in this project and explain how it helped you.

Something I learned that helped me

....

....

How did we help each other in our group?

Marcus is thinking about how the members of his group helped each other during their project.

It was really helpful looking at information sources together. It was nice having Sofia explain some new words to me! Some of the texts we had to read were quite complicated.

Work with your group. Think about all the activities you have completed together. Talk about the things you did to help each other, then answer the questions.

1 What helpful thing did each person in the group do to help make your information book?

Name	How they helped
....	....
....	....
....	....
....	....
....	....

Look at these questions and circle the best symbol for you.

a How well did the group work together?   ★   ☺   ☺

b Do you think your group was successful in your task to tell other children about healthy eating?   ★   ☺   ☺

c Explain your reason: ....

2 Ask your group to help you complete this sentence.

My group thought it was helpful when I ....

3 Complete this sentence by yourself.

My group helped me to ....

What can we tell each other about what we have learned?

Talk with a partner from your group.

sk them to look at these statements and (circle) the best symbol for you.

How well does your partner think that you:

a listened to others in the group? ★ ☺ 😐

b made some helpful suggestions? ★ ☺ 😐

c helped the group to agree? ★ ☺ 😐

What have we learned?

Look back over your learning goals in this project. Finish these sentences.

In this project I learned how to ....

Something I did well in this project was ....

Next time I want to be able to ....

3 > Can we learn outside school?

Getting started

Answer the questions with a partner:

a   What can you see in the picture?

b   What do you think Marcus and Zara might be thinking?

c   Do you know any older adults who have learned to do something new?

d   How can people learn things when they are too old to go to school?

Zara

Marcus

LEARN ALL
YOUR LIFE
Use your
local library

> 3.1 What can we learn when we are not in school?

Our learning goals	I think	My teacher thinks
I can use data in a graph or chart to answer questions.	★ ☺ 😐	★ ☺ 😐 ....
I can think of something I could do to make a difference to other people.	★ ☺ 😐	★ ☺ 😐 ....

Learning goals

What sort of skills can we learn outside school?

1   You learn lots of things in school. What kinds of things do you learn when you are **not** in school? Talk with your partner.

How to cook food

How to play a musical instrument or sing

How to draw or make something

How to speak another language

How to do a sport

Something else?

How to play a game

2 Adults also have to learn all the things they need to know. They need to know how to do things for home and for work. Are any of the adults in your family learning? Can you say what they are learning to do?

3 Sofia and Arun are talking about what they do when they are not in school.

I have swimming lessons on Wednesdays and I go to the library on Saturdays. I like the non-fiction section best.

On Tuesdays, I go to judo, and I have a violin lesson on Thursdays.

Sofia and her group asked their classmates what learning activities they do when they are not at school. They recorded their results in a **pictogram**. Look carefully at their pictogram and answer the questions below it.

pictogram

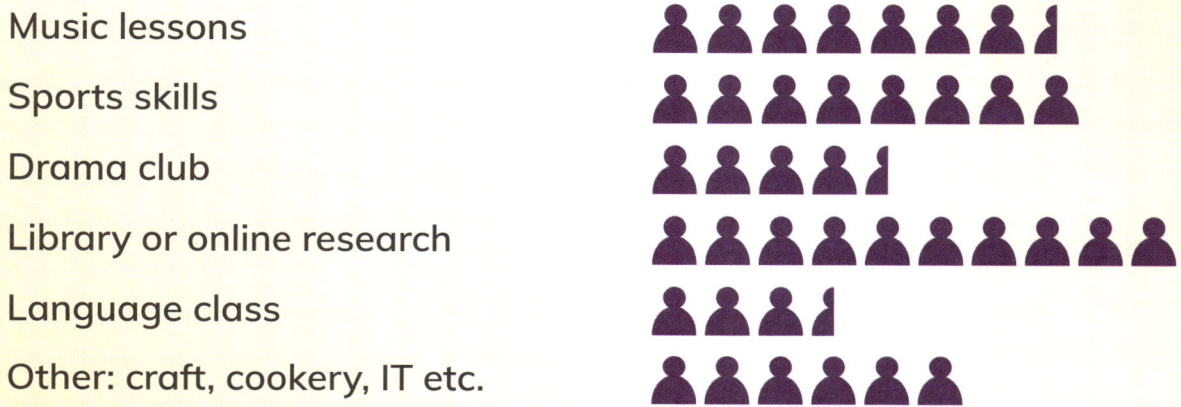

= 2 children

How many children do different activities each week?

Music lessons

Sports skills

Drama club

Library or online research

Language class

Other: craft, cookery, IT etc.

Answer these questions:

a   What is the most popular learning activity outside school?

....

b   How many children go to drama club? ....

c   Do more children have language or music lessons? ....

4   The pictogram showed Sofia and Arun that children in their class do lots of learning activities outside school. Next, they wanted to find out how much time children spend doing these activities. So they carried out another survey and recorded their results in a **bar chart**.

bar chart

Look carefully at their bar chart and answer the questions below it. (There are 30 children in Sofia and Arun's class.)

How long do children spend on learning activities each week?

a   What is the most common amount of time spent on learning

activities? ....

b   What is the least common amount of time spent on learning

activities? ....

c   How many children did they ask? ....

5   Sofia and Arun looked at their bar chart and thought about what they could learn from the results. They wrote their **conclusions**. Tick the ones that are correct.

conclusion

1. Most children in our class do learning activities outside school. ☐

2. Lots of us spend 3 hours per week learning sports skills. ☐

3. Most of us spend more than 4 hours per week on learning activities outside school. ☐

4. Most of us spend 1–3 hours per week on learning activities outside school. ☐

Did you know?

Did you know that between 25 and 30 million children around the world go to a chess class every week?

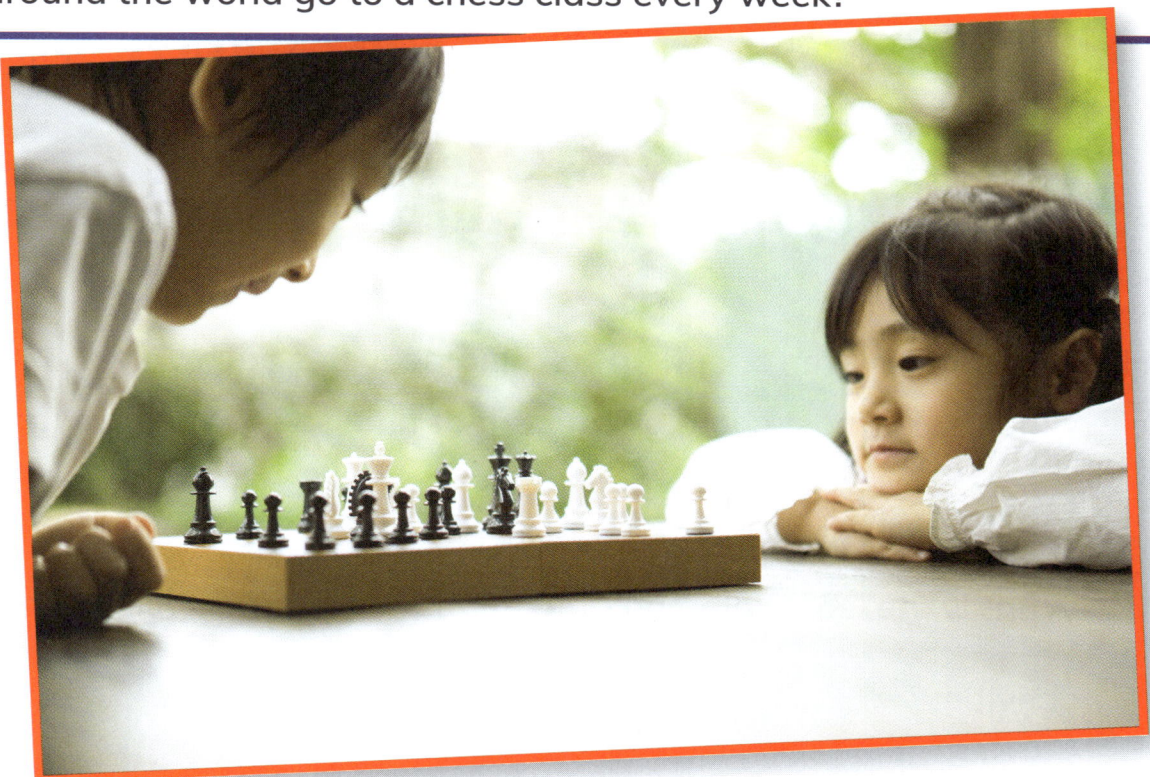

How can we find out about places to learn in our area?

Arun wants to find out where there are places to learn in his area: District 5 in the town of Westside. He found this **GPS map** online.

He notices that there are different kinds of places to learn: places where children have to go to learn and other places where people can go to learn new skills if they want to.

GPS map

1   Arun has made a table and started adding the different learning places from the map. Work with a partner to finish the table by writing down some of these places.

Schools	Places to learn different skills
District 5 Primary School	District 5 Community Centre
....	....
....	....

2 How many learning places in your local area do you know of?
With your group, make a copy of Arun's table.
List as many places as you can in your area.

Then look at a map of your local area. Can you find your school?
Can you find some of the other places you wrote on your list?

3 Talk about the questions, then finish the sentences together.
The words in the box may help you.

How can we find out more about learning places in our area?

How can we find out what our classmates learn outside school?

How can we find out where our family members go to learn things?

Does our learning help other people?

What do children in other places learn

researching online   doing a class survey   looking at a map

talking to them   making a questionnaire

1. We will find out where there are places to learn in our area

   by ....

2. We will find out what our classmates do by

   ....

3. We will find out where other people in our families go to

   learn by ....

4   With your group, talk about how you could tell other people about places to learn in your area. How do you think this will help them?

Finish these sentences:

We could find out if our learning helps others by

....

We could find out what children in other places learn by

....

Top tip

If you find out about more local learning places, add them to your list.

› 3.2 How can we look for places to learn outside school?

Learning goals

Our learning goals	I think	My teacher thinks
I can make up my own questions to help me find out about an issue.	★ ☺ ☐	★ ☺ ☐ ....
I can carry out an investigation using my own questions.	★ ☺ ☐	★ ☺ ☐ ....

Our learning goals	I think	My teacher thinks
I can use a simple chart to record the results of my research.	★ ☺ ☺	★ ☺ ☺ ....

What questions can we ask children in our class about learning activities?

Sofia's group have found out some facts about what their classmates learn outside school.

They have found out:

- which learning activities their classmates do

- how many hours their classmates spend doing learning activities each week.

Now they want to find out some more information.
They think it will be easier to record the information
if they ask questions that will have a number in the answer.

1   Look at the questions they have thought of.
Tick (✓)the ones that would have a number as an answer.

1   Do you have swimming lessons at the Westside Pool? ☐

2   How often do you have swimming lessons? ☐

3   Can you talk about all the things you like about Drama Club? ☐

4   How many times per week do you go to the library? ☐

5   How long do you spend at Drama Club each week? ☐

2 Think of three questions to ask your classmates to find out what learning they do outside your school day.
Think of questions that will have a number in the answer.

> How often...?   How long...?
>   How many...?

Top tip

Think of questions that are relevant to your area.

Write your ideas here:

Question:
1 ....
2 ....
3 ....

How can we record information about places to learn?

1 Choose one of your questions to ask your classmates.

2 Look at the three examples of **frequency tables** and decide which one you will use to record your **data** in. Think about which one will fit the question you have chosen.

> **frequency table**
>
> **data**
>
> **row**
>
> **column**

1

Number of learning activities

Number of activities	Tally of children	Total number of children
0		
1		
2		
3		
4+		

2

Number of times done each week

Number of times a week	Tally of children	Total of children
0		
1		
2		
3		
4		
5+		

3

Number of hours spent each week

Number of hours a week	Tally of children	Total of children
0–1		
1–2		
2–3		
3–4		
4–5		
5+		

The best table for me to record my data is table number ....

3 Copy the table you have chosen (you will need to add more **rows**). Write the heading at the top of the first **column**. Write the numbers in the first column.

Top tip

You can look on page 16 for information on how to do a tally!

Write the correct heading for your table here.

	Tally of children	Total of children

4 Now ask 15 children your question and record their answers in your table.

What have we found out?

Marcus wants to make a bar chart to show the results of his survey. He has started making his bar chart, but he is not sure what to do next. He asks Sofia to help him.

Top tip

A bar chart has a **horizontal axis** (along the bottom) and a **vertical** axis (up the side).

horizontal

axis

vertical

91

Title: ....

Number of ....

3 1 Read the questions below. Then listen to what Sofia
      says to Marcus. Listen out for the answers to the questions.

   a What question did Marcus ask in his survey?

   b In his bar chart, what will the **vertical** axis show?

   c What will the **horizontal** axis show in Marcus's chart?

   d How many different numbers will Marcus need to write
      on his horizontal axis?

   2 Now you are going to make a bar chart to show what you
      have found out from your research. You can copy Marcus's table,
      but you will probably need to add more rows.

   a Use the question you asked your classmates as the title
      for your bar chart.

   b Use the headings from your frequency table to label the axes.
      Write the number of children on the vertical axis.

   c Count the total number of children in each section of your frequency
      table. Colour in the right number of bars on your chart.

3   When you have finished making your bar chart, answer these questions about it.

    a   What does the highest bar in your chart show you?

....

    b   What does the lowest bar on your chart tell you?

....

    c   How many children did you ask? ....

> 3.3 What can adults teach children outside school?

Learning goals		
Our learning goals	**I think**	**My teacher thinks**
I can give reasons for my opinion about an issue.	★ ☺ 😐	★ ☺ 😐 ....
I can find information and answers to questions in a source.	★ ☺ 😐	★ ☺ 😐 ....

What difference can extra learning make to people's lives?

People can learn new skills throughout their lives. We call it lifelong learning. They have hobbies that they learned to do for fun.

Some adults have to learn special skills to get the right qualifications for their type of work.

> lifelong learning
>
> hobby
>
> qualification

1   You are going to watch a video. You will hear four adults talking about the special skills they have learned.
Watch the video, then answer the questions about each person.

The gardener

a   What special knowledge does the gardener need to have?

....

....

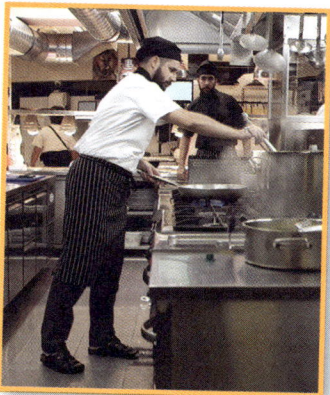

The chef

b   Where did the chef learn to cook?

....

....

The chess player

c   Who taught the chess player to play?

....

....

The violin player

d   Who is the violin player helping?

....

....

2   Discuss these questions in your group. Write down the answers.

a   Which adult said they helped other adults to teach children?

the gardener

the chef

the chess player

the violin player

b   What difference does extra learning make to the people in the video?
Circle your opinion.

a lot   a little   none

Explain your answer ....

....

How can we find out what people think about learning activities?

Zara and Marcus decide to find out more about the learning
activities that people can do in their area, District 5 in Westside.
They start looking at some different sources.

I've found a report in the newspaper about lifelong learning. Shall we read it?

Maybe, but first let's think about what kind of information we need.

They write some questions.

Does it give us information about learning in our area (District 5 in Westside)?

Does it give us information about what courses you can do and where you can do them?

1   With your group, look at the five sources that Zara and Marcus have found. Answer these questions about them.

   a   Which source was written by adults telling children they will have fun learning something new?

   ....

   b   Which source was written by someone who knows how to 'catch air'?

   ....

   c   Do any sources encourage people to do something that

   will help others? ....

   Explain your answer. ....

   ....

   ....

Skate boarding in the park

24 May 14:06

Hey everyone!

Want to do some cool skateboard stuff?

Come and catch air with me at Westside Skateboard Park every Wednesday, from 4–6pm.

2

Westside Observer
Local news for local people

District 5 residents are the happiest in Westside

A new report into the benefits of lifelong learning has just been published, and the residents of District 5 have come out top of the whole city of Westside!

3

District 5
Community Centre Newsletter

What's on at your local community centre this month?

Monday and Wednesday 10 a.m. to midday

Feel Alive in District 5

A gentle exercise class for the over 70s.

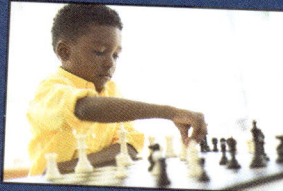

Tuesday and Thursday 4–6 p.m.

Kids' Chess Club

All levels welcome.

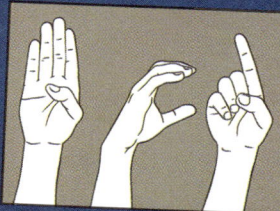

Wednesday 4–6 p.m.

Learn Sign Language

A class for adults and children (age 10+) working towards their Grade 2 qualification.

Sunday 10 a.m. to 1 p.m.

Digital photography for children (ages 7+)

Learn how to hold a digital camera to take close ups and wide-angle shots. Find out how to use different settings and editing tools to make your photos look even better.

4

Music lessons for kids

Choose an instrument:

violin   dhol   flute   keyboard

Learn to play at our studios
in District 5 Music Hub.

We make learning a new instrument fun!

5

Looking for a new adventure?

Come and volunteer at
District 5 Community Gardens!

- Make new friends.
- Learn how to grow and look after plants.
- Help keep our gardens an enjoyable space for everyone.

Everyone is welcome – whatever their age!

2 Look again at the sources about learning activities that you can do in District 5, Westside – Zara and Marcus's area. Write the numbers of these sources in the table. Complete the table by putting ✓ or ✗ in each column.

Source number	Can children do the activities?	Are there activities to help you get better at something?	Are there activities that help other people?	Do the sources make the activities sound like something you would like to do?

Top tip

Look for words that tell you **where** a place is, **who** it is
for and **what** it is like to do the activity.

3 Look at your completed table and answer the questions.

a How many sources give information about activities for children?

....

b How many sources give information about activities that help you

to get better at something? ....

c How many sources make the activities sound like you would want

to do them? ....

› 3.4 How can we show other children about places to learn in our area?

Learning goals

Our learning goals	I think	My teacher thinks
I can identify what tasks each group member will do.	★ ☺ 😐	★ ☺ 😐 ....
I can work well with other group members to achieve our group's goal.	★ ☺ 😐	★ ☺ 😐 ....

How can we work together in our group?

You are going to work with your group to make a map display. Your display will show children different places where people can learn in your area.

information panel

key

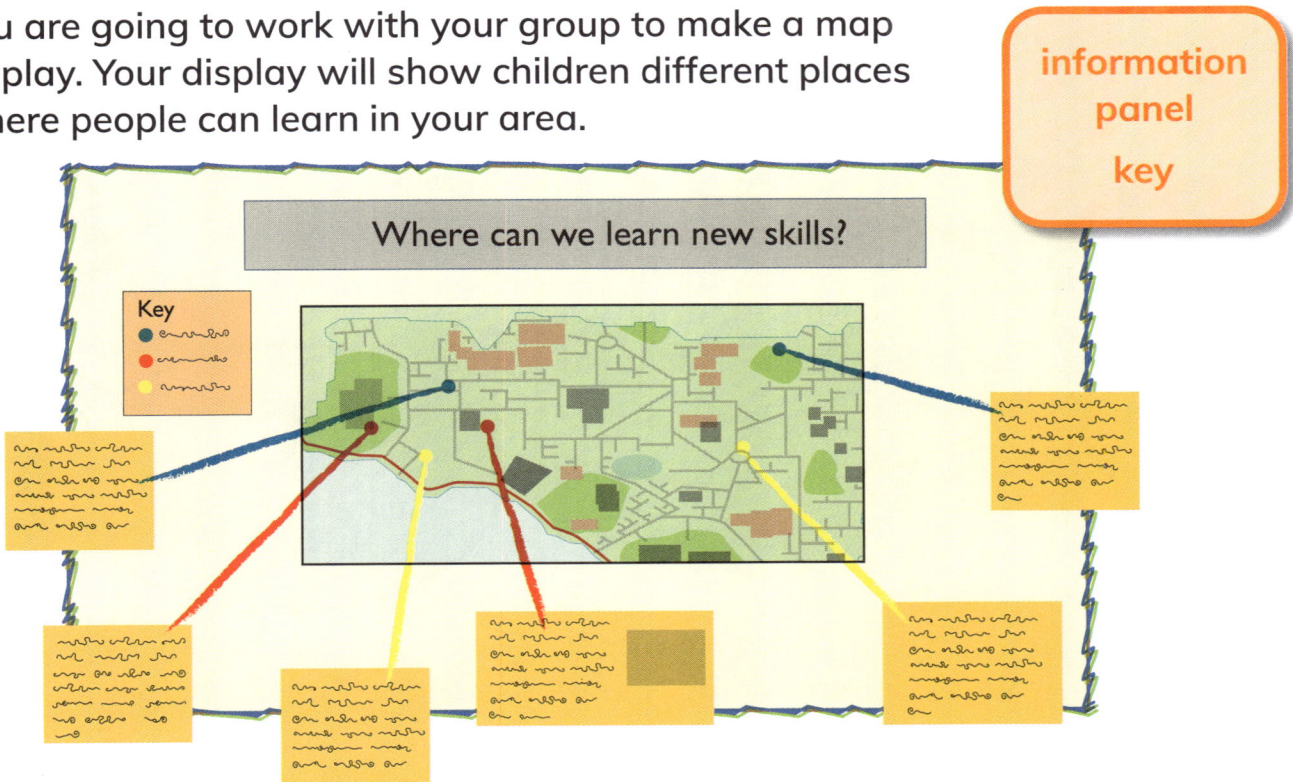

Zara and her group are planning their display.

They have thought about what information will appear on and around their map of their local area and how they can work together. They made a list of their ideas:

Our group's map display plan

How we can show places to learn in our area
(by Zara, Arun, Marcus and Sofia)

1   Map of District 5 so that we can show where places are
2   **Information panels** about different learning places to put around the map
3   A colour-coded **key** to identify different places on the map
4   String to link the information to each learning place on the map

1 Look at the picture of the display.
Find and point to the features from Zara's group's display plan.

2 Zara's group decide to do some research to find out more
details about the different places to learn in District 5,
the area where they live in the city of Westside.

> I think we can get the information we need by looking for answers to five questions.

> Yes, we can ask 'who', 'what', 'where', 'when' and 'why'.

Write **who**, **what**, **where**, **when** and **why** in the correct box to show
what sort of information each question will help you to collect:

Question	To find out:
1	The type of learning that happens in a place.
2	The times that classes happen.
3	The people the class is suitable for (ages: adults, children, all).
4	The location of the learning place.
5	The reason to do the course: new skills or a qualification?

3 Work with your group. Look at the list of learning places in your area that you made with your group. Make sure you can find the places on your map of your local area.

Discuss and make notes:

- Which learning places in your area do you want to put in your display?
- How can you get information about these learning places?
- How will you show where each place is on the map?
- Who will be responsible for the information panel about each learning place?

Fill in the map display plan.

Our group's map display plan.

Learning place information panel   Name of group member

....

....

....

....

....

....

....

Did you know?

You can learn something new and help others at the same time. Community groups can ask for volunteers to help collect food and clothes for others, or tidy up the local area with litter picking or weeding. These sorts of activities help us learn about caring for other people.

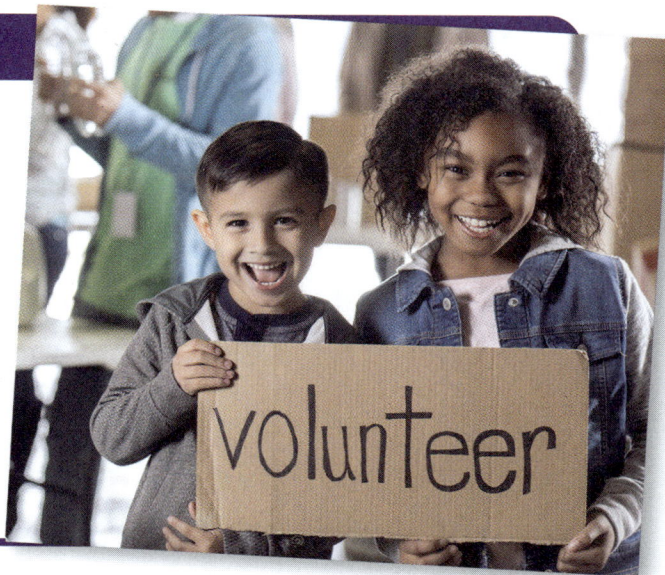

What will our map display look like?

1   Work with your group.
    Talk about how you want your finished map display to look.

   • Will you write your information panels by hand or will you print them?

   • What pictures or photos will you include?

   • What will the title of your display be?

Top tip

You could use colours to show the different kinds of places on your map. For example, you could use red for places where adults learn, blue for places where children learn, green for sports, yellow for music, etc. You will need to make a key to tell people what the different colours mean.

2   Draw a plan of your display on a piece of paper and label each part that you will include.

3   Follow these stages to develop your map display.

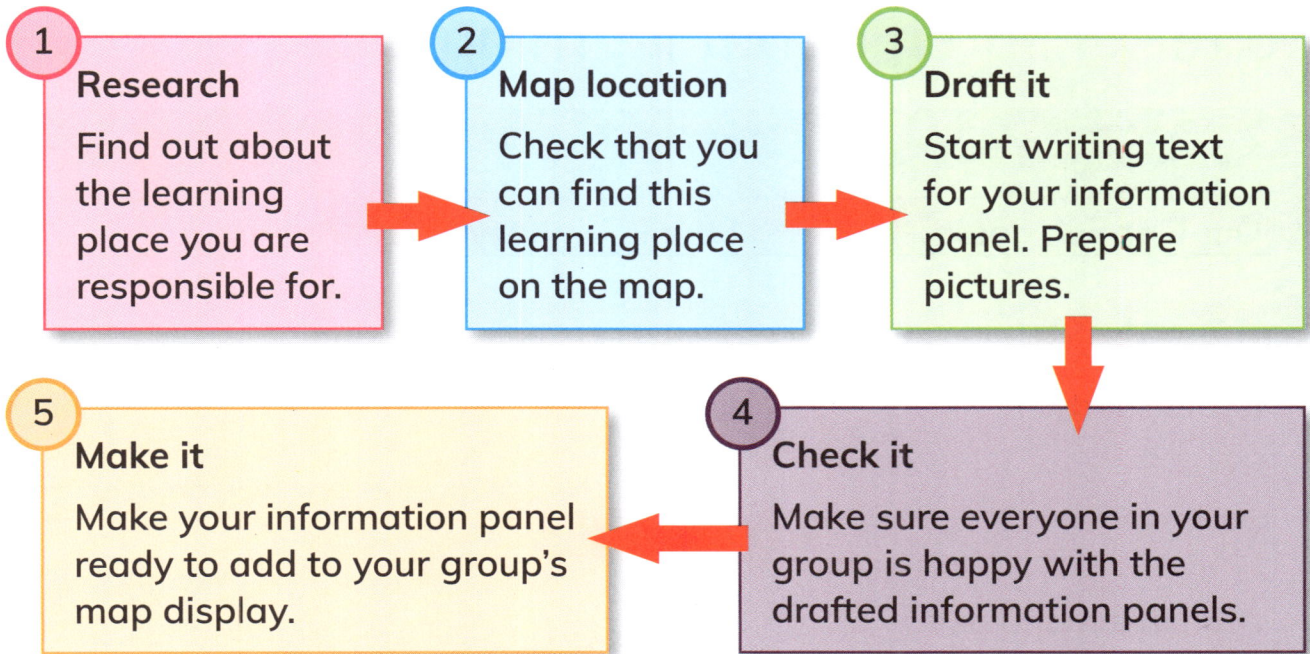

1 **Research**
Find out about the learning place you are responsible for.

→

2 **Map location**
Check that you can find this learning place on the map.

→

3 **Draft it**
Start writing text for your information panel. Prepare pictures.

↓

5 **Make it**
Make your information panel ready to add to your group's map display.

←

4 **Check it**
Make sure everyone in your group is happy with the drafted information panels.

❭ 3.5 How can we use our map display to tell children about learning places?

Learning goals

Our learning goals	I think	My teacher thinks
I can talk about an issue clearly.	★ ☺ 😐	★ ☺ 😐 ....
I can listen and ask relevant questions.	★ ☺ 😐	★ ☺ 😐 ....

How will we display our map and information about local learning places?

We need to check where to put each part.

We need to make sure there's room for everything. It needs to look good so people will want to read it.

1   Work with your group. Check the plan that you made
and talk about how you want your finished display to look.
The diagram will help you decide how to lay out your display.

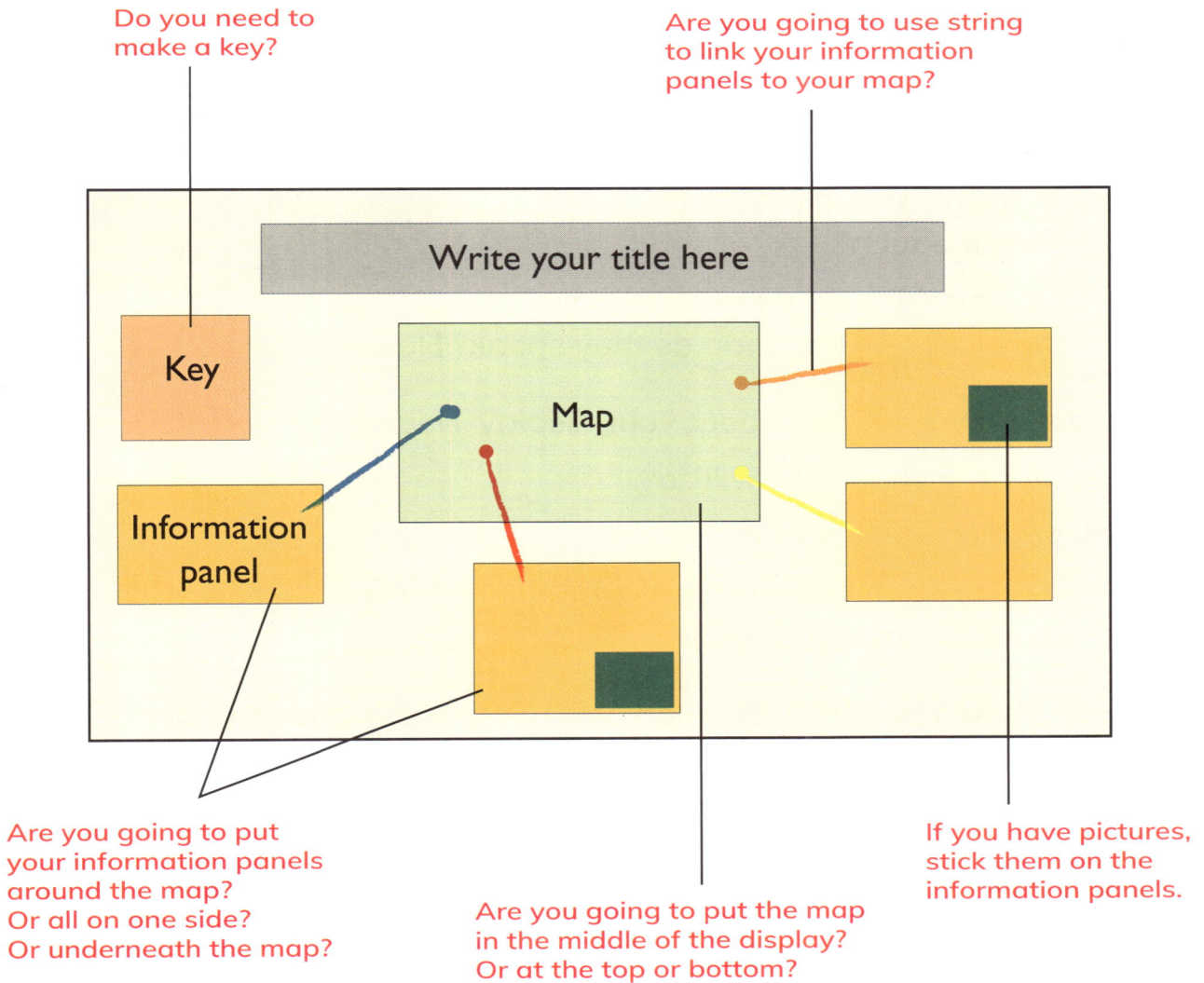

Do you need to
make a key?

Are you going to use string
to link your information
panels to your map?

Write your title here

Key

Map

Information
panel

Are you going to put
your information panels
around the map?
Or all on one side?
Or underneath the map?

Are you going to put the map
in the middle of the display?
Or at the top or bottom?

If you have pictures,
stick them on the
information panels.

2   Collect all the things you
need to put your display
together.

Top tip

Before you glue the parts of your display,
lay everything out in the positions you
have agreed and make sure everyone
in your group is happy with the effect.

How will we present our displays to other children in our class?

1 Sofia, Marcus, Arun and Zara have finished their map display.
Listen as they present it to some classmates. Answer the questions.

   a Which learning places do they mention?

   b Do you think they are pointing to things on their map as they speak? How can you tell?

2 Talk with your group about your display. Decide:

   • what each person will say

   • in what order you will speak

   • what you will do to keep your audience interested in what you are saying.

3 How should you behave when another group is presenting their display to you? Look at these rules. Put a tick ✓ next to the good rules and a cross ✗ next to the ones that are not good.

   a Look at the person who is speaking. ☐

   b Interrupt the person who is speaking. ☐

   c Ask relevant questions at the right time. ☐

   d Read your book while another group is speaking. ☐

   e Politely suggest any improvements you think they could make. ☐

4 Take it in turns with your classmates to show and talk about your map display and listen to other groups.

Can we improve our map display?

Arun and Zara are talking about their map display and how they shared it with other children.

> It was a good idea to make a key with different colours for each type of learning place. That worked well.

> When we talked, we could have made it clearer that these places are really close to our school.

What worked well when you presented your display to the class?

What could you improve? Talk with your group. Record your ideas here:

The best thing about our display is ....

....

Our display could be even better if ....

....

> 3.6 What have we learned during this project?

Learning goals

Our learning goals	I think	My teacher thinks
I can describe something good I did as a member of a group.	★ ☺ ☺	★ ☺ ☺ ....
I can describe something I could do better as a member of a group next time.	★ ☺ ☺	★ ☺ ☺ ....
I can describe how working as a team helped us to achieve our goal.	★ ☺ ☺	★ ☺ ☺ ....

How well did I work in my group?

Zara and Marcus are reflecting on their project work. They are talking about how the group decided what information to collect.

Marcus, you suggested using who, what, where, when, why to find the information we needed. That was a really good idea.

Thanks, but I think I could have been a better listener – you and Arun had good ideas too.

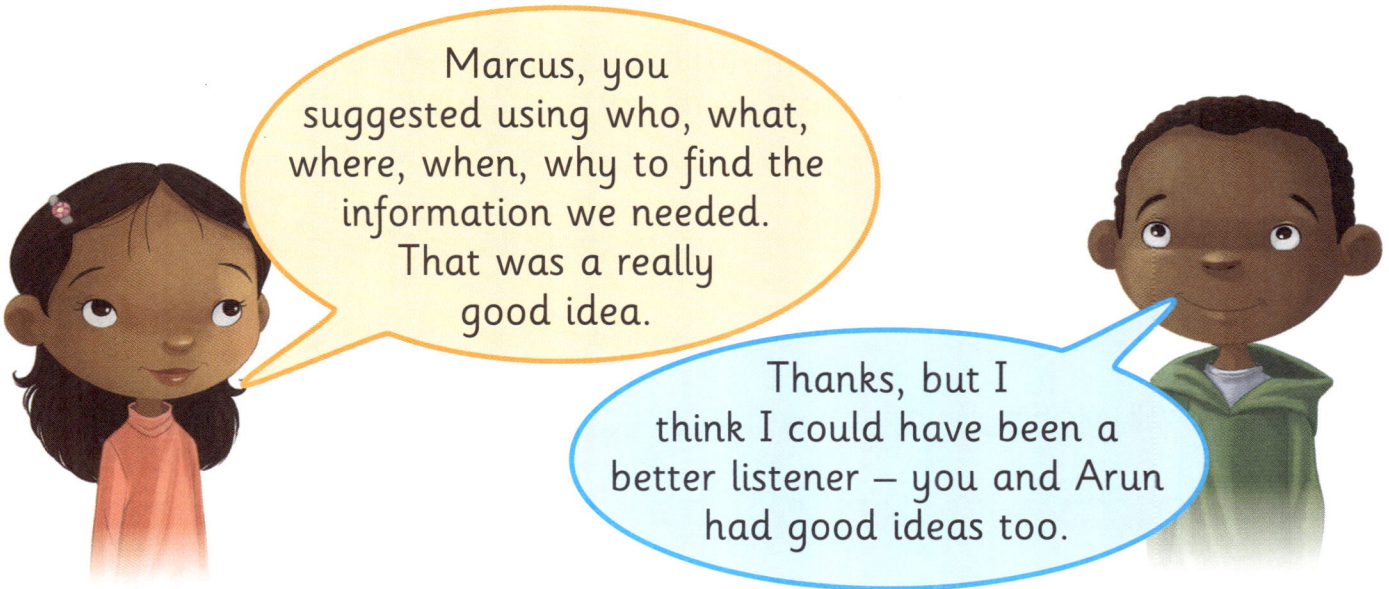

1   Think about the work you did for your group's project and answer these questions.

   a   The information panel I worked on was about: ....

   ....

   b   Choose from this list or describe some of the other ways you helped to make your group's map display look good:

   > drawing a picture   writing titles
   >
   > attaching the labels   helping someone

   A good idea that I had

   ....

   Something I did to make our display look good

   ....

   Some useful research that I did

   ....

2 Marcus thinks he could be a better listener next time. What do you think you could do better next time?

> <u>Something I would like to do better next time</u>
>
> Next time, I hope to ....
>
> This will help my group because ....

How did we help each other in our group?

Arun and Sofia are thinking about how their group helped each other during the project.

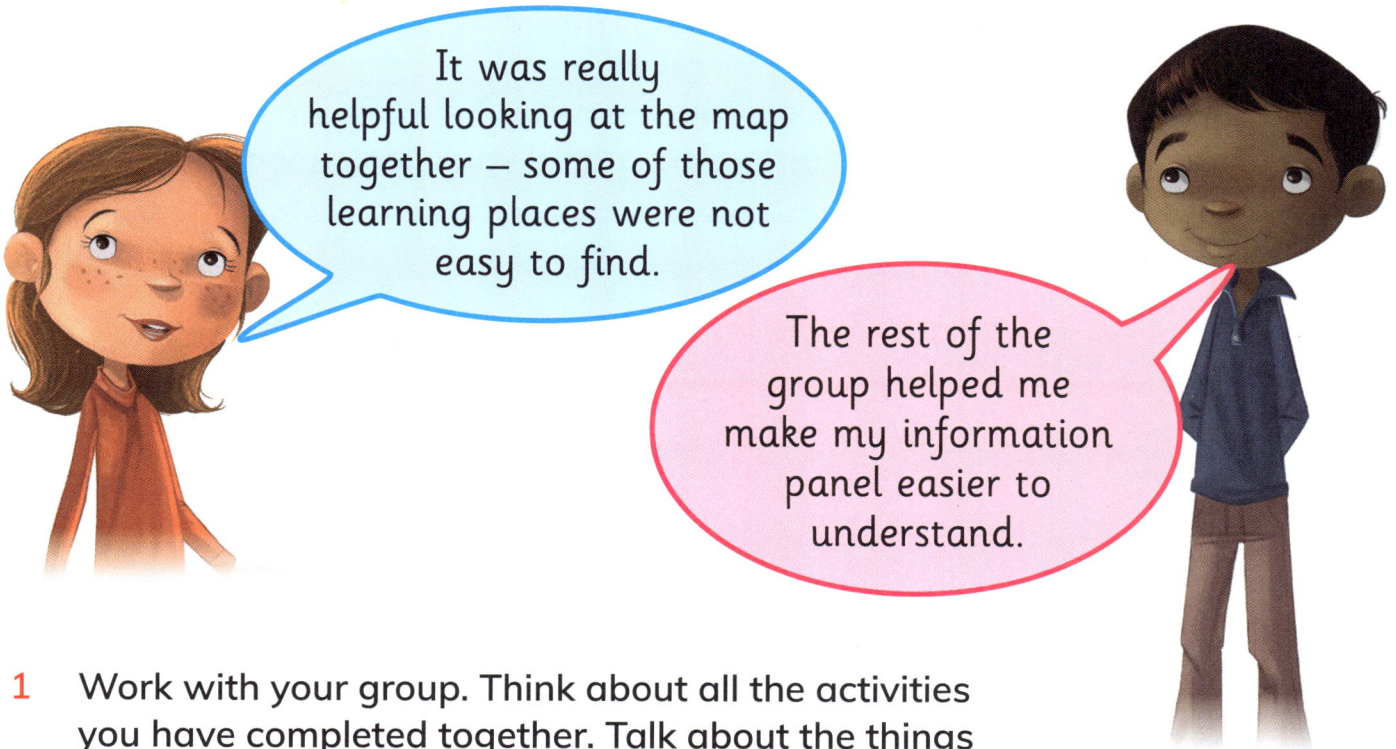

It was really helpful looking at the map together – some of those learning places were not easy to find.

The rest of the group helped me make my information panel easier to understand.

1 Work with your group. Think about all the activities you have completed together. Talk about the things you did to help each other, then complete the sentences.

My group thought it was helpful when I ....

My group helped me to ....

I learned about being a good group member by ....

2 How did working as a team help your group to finish your project?

....

Do you think your group was successful in your task? **Yes   No**
Explain your answer.

....

What can we tell each other about what we have learned?

Talk with a partner from your group.
Ask them to look at these statements and (circle) the best symbol for you.
How well does your partner think that you:

a   listened to others in the group?   ★   ☺   😐

b   made some helpful suggestions?   ★   ☺   😐

c   helped the group to agree?   ★   ☺   😐

What have we learned?

Now look back over your learning goals in this project and finish these sentences:

In this project I learned how to ....

Something I did well on this project was ....

Something I need to keep improving is ....

4 ▶ How can we look after our oceans?

viewing window

Getting started

Answer the questions with a partner:

a   Sofia, Arun, Zara and Marcus are visiting an aquarium. Describe what you can see.

b   What do you know about oceans and ocean creatures?

c   How much of the Earth do you think is covered by water?

d   Why do we need to look after the oceans?

globe

Zara

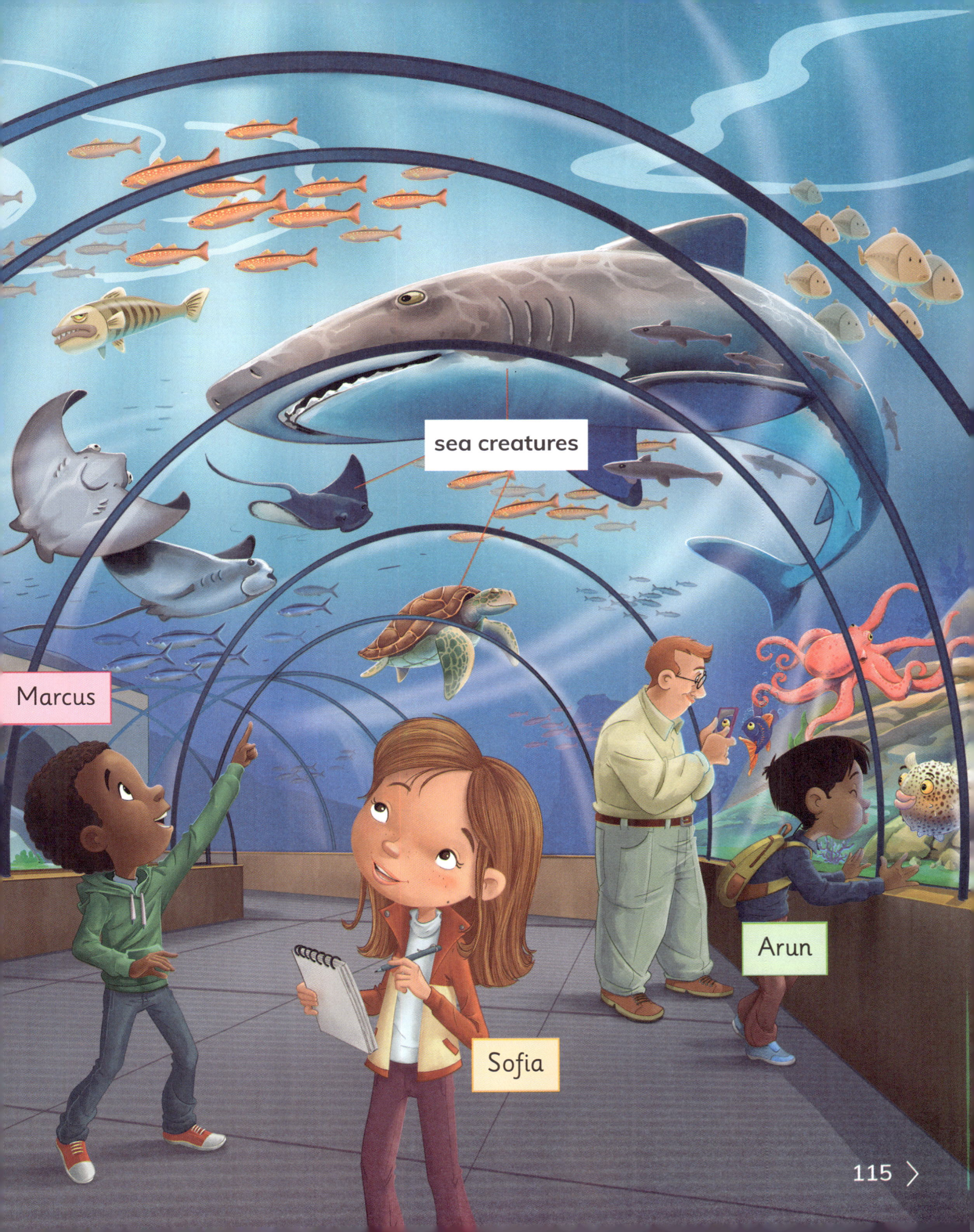

sea creatures

Marcus

Sofia

Arun

> 4.1 Why do we need to look after the oceans?

Learning goals		
Our learning goals	**I think**	**My teacher thinks**
I can find information and answers to questions in a source.	★ ☺ ☺	★ ☺ ☺ ....
I can use data in a chart to answer questions.	★ ☺ ☺	★ ☺ ☺ ....
I can use a simple chart or diagram to record the results of my research.	★ ☺ ☺	★ ☺ ☺ ....

What can we find out about oceans?

Sofia and Marcus picked up a leaflet when they visited the aquarium. Read the leaflet and answer the questions.

Why are oceans important?

Oceans cover around three-quarters of the planet.

We all need oxygen to breathe. Over 50 percent of our planet's oxygen is produced by tiny plants in the oceans.

Hundreds of thousands of different species of animals live in the ocean.

Around a billion people in the world depend on fish as a source of protein.

Nearly 40 million people have a job which depends on the sea.

Are the oceans clean?

Plastic pollution is one of the biggest problems affecting oceans, around 8 million tonnes of plastic end up in the oceans every year.

Around 40 percent of the ocean's surface is covered with plastic rubbish.

Most plastics in the ocean break down into very small pieces called microplastics. Scientists estimate there are now 2.3 million tonnes of microplastic in our oceans.

If we carry on, there will soon be more plastic than fish in the ocean.

oxygen   rubbish

1   How much of the Earth's surface is covered by oceans? Tick (✓) one box:

around 100% ☐   around 75% ☐   around 50% ☐   around 25% ☐

2   What can you see in the photo of a turtle that does not belong

in the ocean? ....

3   What are 'microplastics'? ....

4   Tick (✓) one box:

If we don't stop throwing away
plastic, there will soon be ...

more fish than plastic   ☐

more whales than people   ☐

more plastic than fish   ☐

more fish than scientists   ☐

Did you know?

The blue whale is the largest animal that has ever lived on Earth. It can grow to over 30 metres long and it can weigh as much as 180,000 kilograms. Its tongue weighs about the same as an elephant and its heart is the size of a car!

What does the data show us about pollution in the oceans?

Marcus did some research online to find out more about pollution in the oceans. He found a **pie chart** that shows the **proportions** of some of the most common types of rubbish in the water.

pie chart

proportion

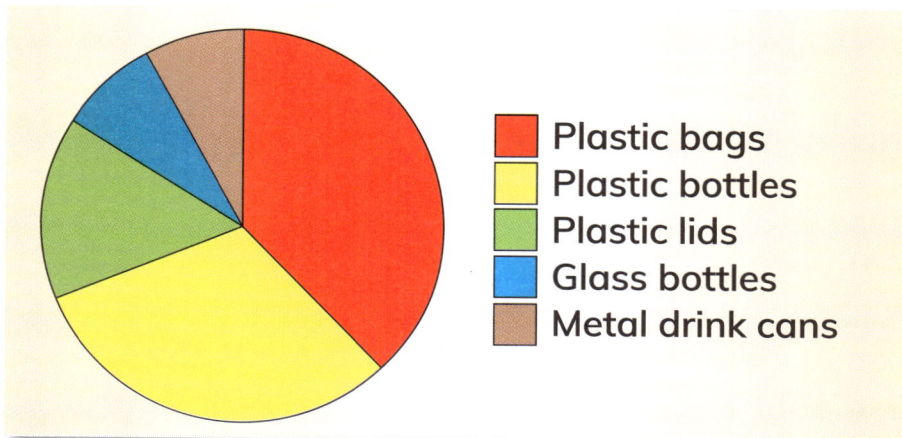

Plastic bags
Plastic bottles
Plastic lids
Glass bottles
Metal drink cans

Top tip

Look at the size of each slice in the pie chart to help you answer the questions.

Talk to your partner about the information in the pie chart.
Answer the questions:

a   What three materials are named in the pie chart?

....

b   What is the most common type of rubbish found in the ocean,

according to the pie chart? ....

c   Which is there more of in our oceans: plastic bottles

or glass bottles? ....

Why is there so much plastic in the oceans?

Arun and Zara are talking about the pie chart information.

There seems to be so much more plastic than any other sort of rubbish.

Is it because people throw away more plastic — or something about plastic itself?

Arun and Zara decide to do more research.
They find some more information online.

How long do different kinds of rubbish take to decompose?	
Material	Time it takes to decompose
banana peel	2–5 weeks
paper towel	3–4 weeks
newspaper	6 weeks
cardboard box	2 months
cotton shirt	2–5 months
plastic bag	10–20 years
rubber boot	50–80 years
aluminium can	200 years
plastic cup	400 years
plastic bottle	450 years

1   Use the information about all the materials in the table to complete
    this **Carroll diagram** – the first two have been done for you:

Carroll diagram   decompose

Type of material	0–10 years	Over 10 years
Plastics		Plastic grocery bag
Non-plastics	Paper towel	

2   Look at the Carroll diagram and answer the questions:

a   What types of material take less than 10 years to **decompose**?

....

b   Which types of material take over 10 years to decompose?

....

c   Do any plastics decompose in less than 10 years?
    (Circle) your answer.   Yes   No

d   How long does it take a plastic bottle to decompose?
    Tick (✓) one box:

10 years	80 years	200 years	400 years	450 years

3   Remember the question that Arun and Zara thought about earlier.

> Why is there more plastic than other rubbish in the sea?
> Is it because people throw away more plastic – or is it
> something about plastic itself?

Use the information you have found out about plastic in the
pie chart and in the Carroll diagram to answer the question.
What do you think? Tick (✓) **one** box:
Opinion 1: The large amount of plastic pollution is because
so many things are made of plastic, so people throw away more.
Opinion 2: The large amount of plastic pollution is because
plastic takes so long to decompose.
Opinion 3: There is more than one reason for the large
amount of plastic pollution.
Opinion 4: The large amount of plastic pollution is because
plastic floats.

Explain your answer ....

....

> 4.2 Why is plastic pollution a problem?

Learning goals

Our learning goals	I think	My teacher thinks
I can think about what happens when people do things and how their actions affect others.	★ ☺ 😐	★ ☺ 😐 ....

Where does plastic pollution in the ocean come from?

1   Lots of things are often made from plastic.
    With your partner, tick (✓) the things that you think contain plastic:

a computer ☐   a cricket bat ☐

a packet of crisps ☐   a mobile phone ☐

a bicycle helmet ☐   .... ☐

.... ☐   .... ☐

Think of three more things that contain plastic.
Add them to the list.

Plastic is such a useful material. But sometimes it ends up where it shouldn't be — like in the sea!

2   Arun is thinking about the advantages and disadvantages of plastic.

Watch the video and answer these two questions.

- How does plastic end up in the sea?

- What fact about plastic did you find most surprising?

Share your ideas with your class.

3   You are going to watch the video again. Before you do, read these questions and try to answer them. Then watch the video to see if you were right.

landfill site

a   How much plastic ends up in the ocean every minute? Tick (✓) one box.

One full tuktuk

One full rubbish truck

One full rubbish bag

Two full rubbish bins

b   Where has the plastic in this river come from? Tick (✓) the boxes that apply:

Landfill sites

Overflowing rubbish bins

Anywhere that people leave it

c   Finish this sentence.

When we wash our clothes, tiny pieces of plastic ....

....

d What is **ghost gear**? Tick (✓) one box.

Tiny pieces of plastic from clothes ☐

Old fishing ropes and nets ☐

ghost gear

Did you know?

A lot of plastic is used only once before it is thrown away. We call it 'single-use plastic'. A plastic drinking straw is an example of single-use plastic. How many more examples can you think of?

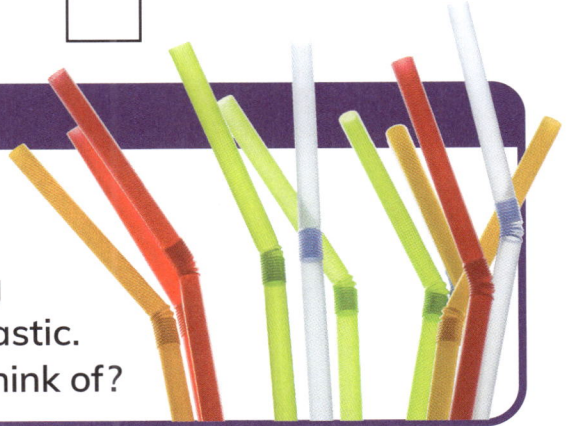

How does plastic pollution in the ocean affect us?

Sofia and Arun are discussing an interesting fact about plastic pollution in the ocean.

current

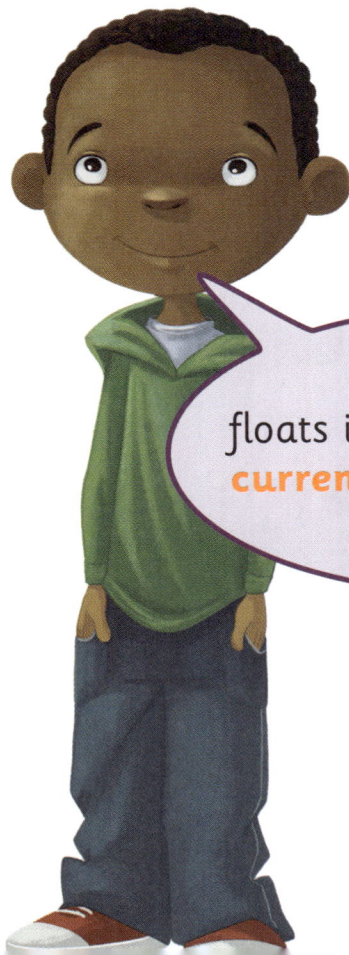

Plastic rubbish floats in water, so the ocean **currents** can carry it a very long distance.

It can even get carried to beaches on islands where nobody lives!

1   Here are some people who have a job that depends on the sea.

marine

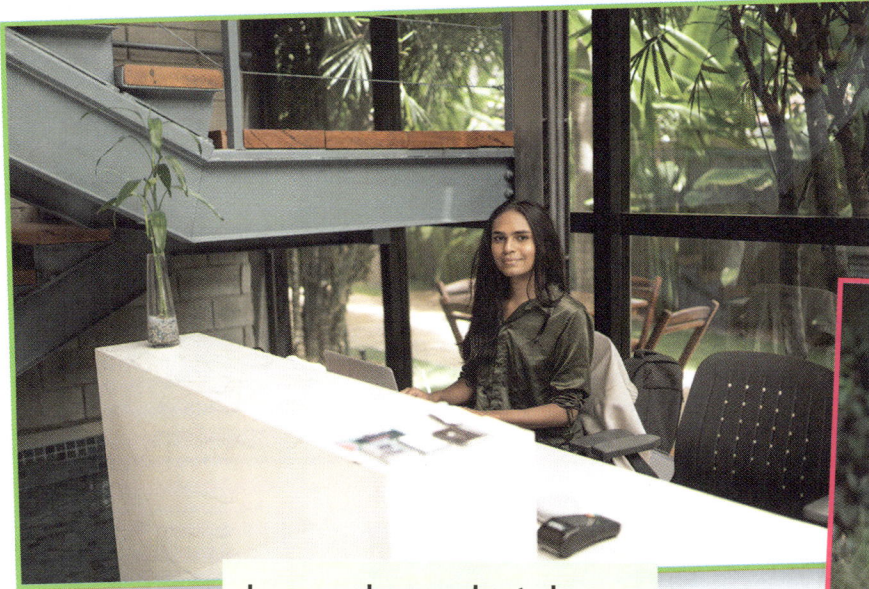

Luana has a hotel next to a lovely beach.

Omar catches fish to sell to people in his village.

Esi is a **marine** scientist. She researches microplastics in the sea.

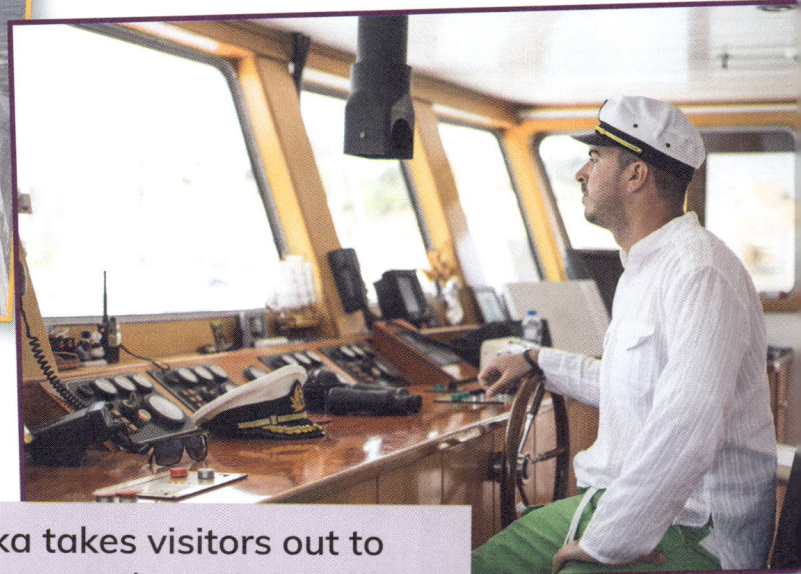

Gorka takes visitors out to sea to watch marine wildlife.

How do you think each person feels about plastic pollution?
Talk with your partner then write the name of each person next
to the speech bubble that gives their point of view.

a It's getting harder and harder to catch fish.

....

....

b No one wants to stay here now there is so much rubbish on the beach.

....

c People pay to see whales and dolphins, not to look at a load of rubbish.

....

d Plants and animals that live in the oceans become unhealthy when there is a large amount of microplastics in the water.

2   Now write the answer to the questions.
    The speech bubbles and the pictures will help you.

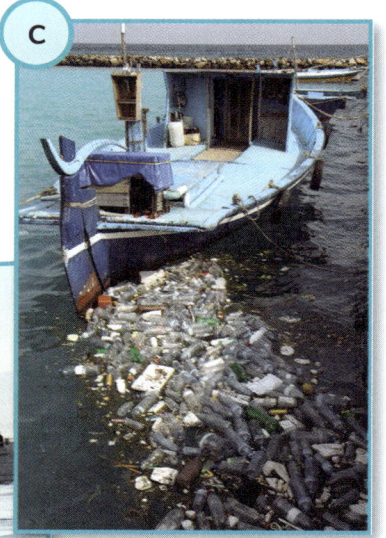

a   Why have people stopped coming to the hotel for holidays?

    ....

    ....

b   Why is it getting harder to earn money from fishing
    and whale watching?

    ....

    ....

c   What makes the plants and animals that live in the oceans
    unhealthy?

    ....

    ....

What can we do about plastic pollution in the ocean?

1   Zara's group thought about what people could do to stop plastic pollution in our oceans.

They started making a list of actions that they think could make a difference. Talk to your group about their ideas, then add three more ideas of your own.

Buy fruit that isn't in a plastic bag.

Don't buy plastic toys that you will only use for one day

....

....

....

Discuss your group's ideas with your class.
Which was your favourite idea?

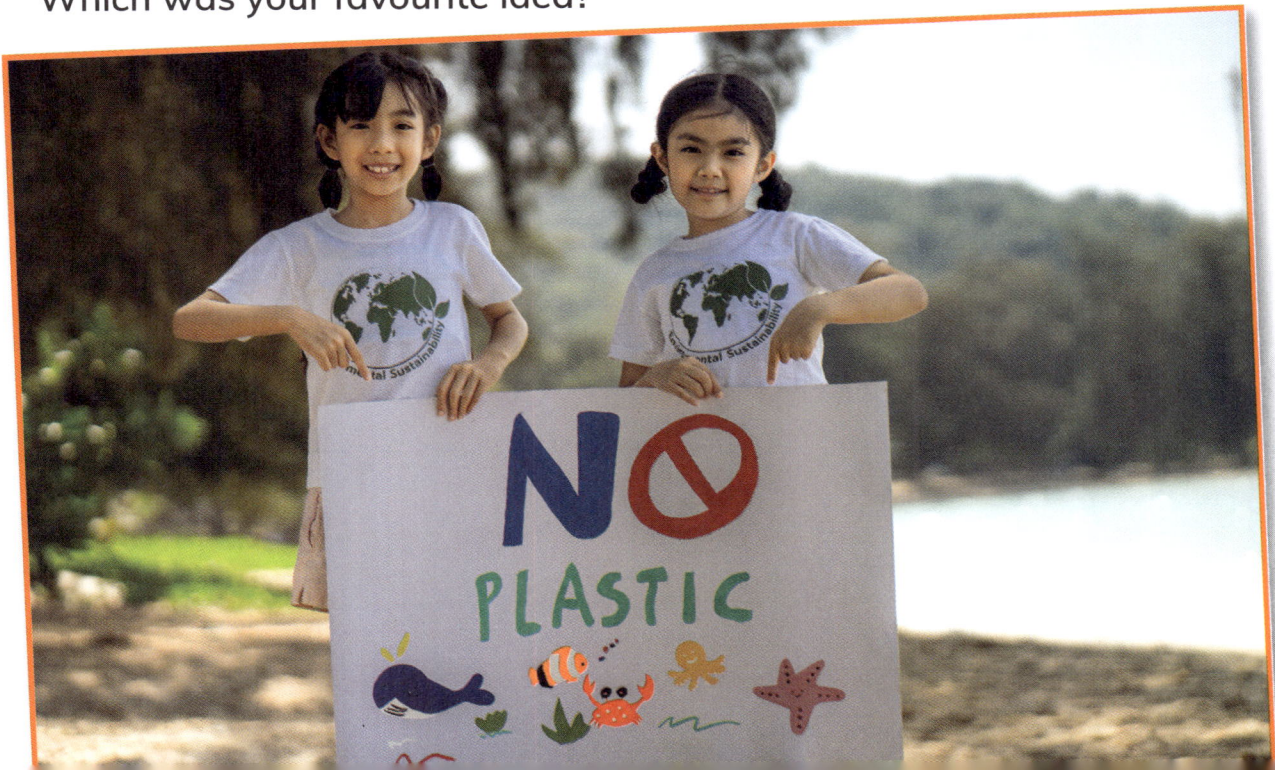

2   Sometimes, if we do one thing, it can lead to another thing. When that thing leads to another thing it can make a **chain reaction**.

chain reaction

Look at this example with a partner:

| If I take my own bag to the supermarket... | → | I won't need to buy a plastic bag. | → | I won't need to throw away my plastic bag. |

| There will be more fish in the sea. | ← | It won't kill any sea creatures. | ← | My plastic bag won't blow away into the sea. |

Can you make up your own chain reaction? The ideas in the box may help you, or you can think of your own ideas.

If I tell people about plastic pollution...

> People will not buy fruit wrapped in plastic.
> People will understand the problem.
> People will throw away less plastic.
> Factories may try to use sustainable materials.
> Shops may see that people don't want fruit in plastic bags.

Copy the chain reaction below and write in your own ideas.

› 4.3 How do people feel about the amount of plastic around us?

Learning goals		
Our learning goals	**I think**	**My teacher thinks**
I can give reasons for my opinion about an issue.	★ ☺ 😐	★ ☺ 😐 ....
I can talk about a source and say what the author's opinion is.	★ ☺ 😐	★ ☺ 😐 ....

Do people have different opinions about plastic pollution?

1   Lots of the ropes and nets that are used to catch fish are made from plastic. They are often thrown away in the sea when they get too old to use. What is this type of pollution called? Tick (✓) one box.

sea gear ▢   ghost gear ▢   shadow gear ▢

2 You are going to hear from two more people who have a job that depends on the sea.

Hadiza works on this large fishing trawler.

Azim works on this small fishing boat.

🎧 5 Listen to what Hadiza and Azim say about old fishing equipment in the ocean. Do they have the same opinion about it? With your partner, talk about what Hadiza and Azim think.

3 Listen again, then write the answers to the questions.

a What do Hadiza and Azim do for a living? Tick (✓) one box.

They are:

marine scientists ☐   fishers ☐   whale-watching guides ☐

b Finish the sentence to show what both Hadiza and Azim agree on:

We have to work quickly to ....

c Hadiza and Azim disagree about throwing old fishing equipment in the ocean. Write the correct name by each opinion:

Opinion 1: Throwing old nets and ropes into the ocean slows us down and cost us time and money. ....

Opinion 2: A few old nets don't cause a problem because the ocean is huge. ....

4   Here are some more opinions. Tick (✓) the one you agree with:

Opinion 3:   Opinion 4:

'Ghost gear' is a problem because marine animals get trapped.

There are so many marine animals, it's not going to make much difference if a few get trapped and die.

Explain your reason for agreeing with this opinion ....

....

5   Why do you think people have different opinions about plastic pollution? Share your ideas with your class.

Where can we find out more about people's opinions on plastic?

1 Work with a partner. Read the newspaper report: it's about collecting plastic that has washed up onto some beaches. Answer the questions together.

reduce

Westside Observer
Local news for local people

Westside Coastal Clean-up

Volunteers from all over Westside join together to take part in the city's coastal clean-up.

Last weekend, hundreds of people who live in Westside went to the city's beaches. They were carrying rubbish bags, litter pickers and gloves. They wanted to clear away washed up plastic pollution.

In one afternoon, volunteers on the District 5 beach collected 50 sacks full of plastic rubbish. Here's what was in them:

- Bits of plastic rope and nets
- Plastic bottles and cups
- Plastic food wrappers

Love Where You Live

The clean-up was organised by the Love Where You Live group

Volunteer helpers cleaning up District 5 beach

who are based in Westside. They wanted to encourage people to care for the environment. Volunteer helper Leena Saad says: 'People get upset when they see litter on our beaches. An event like this helps everyone feel that they are helping'.

District 5 lifeguard Karim De Silva adds: 'It's really important that we keep letting people know how to **reduce** how much plastic they throw away. No one wants to swim in dirty water'.

Local diving teacher Sonia Patel added: 'Clean beaches help everyone who depends on the sea for their job'.

Local ocean scientists hope that even more people will take part in future events. The scientists said: 'This local event can show other places that it's possible to make a difference'.

Not everyone thinks cleaning up the beaches is a good idea. District 2 resident Tom Diamini says: 'What's the point? People will never stop using plastic'.

However, most of the people we spoke to are in favour of using less plastic. Westside Observer will be advertising all future Love Where You Live events. So watch this space!

District 5 beach after the clean-up

a   Find all the opinions that people give in this article.
Underline or highlight them.

b   How many people's opinions did you find? ....

2   Now work on your own to answer these questions.

a   Why did people take part in the clean-up? ....

....

b   What is the name of the group that wants to make a difference

to people's opinions about plastic? ....

c   Look at all the opinions you underlined or highlighted. How many

of these people think the clean-up is a good idea? ....

How many people don't? ....

d   Match these opinions with the person who gave them.

a diving teacher   a volunteer helper

a District 2 resident   a lifeguard

i   People like to do something positive to help. ....

ii   Clean beaches help everyone whose job depends on the sea.

....

iii   People don't like swimming in dirty water. ....

iv   Clean-ups are a waste of time. ....

What have we found out about opinions for and against using plastic?

Zara and Arun are talking about people's opinions in the Westside Observer article.

The newspaper report has lots of opinions from people who think plastic is a problem.

They make some good points, but I'd like to hear some different points of view, too.

1   Here are some more points of view about plastic.
Decide if they are 'for' or 'against' the use of plastic.
Circle the word that describes the point of view best.

1

Lots of people work in factories which make plastics: what will happen to them if the factories stop making plastic?

for   against

2

Lots of people work in jobs that rely on tourists: what will happen if plastic pollution stops people from visiting?

for   against

3

Plastic is very convenient. It is used for all kinds of things that need to be light and easy to clean.

for   against

4

Plastic is cheap, so it doesn't matter if we use plastic things only once and then throw them away.

for   against

5

Single-use plastic is light, so the wind can blow it into the sea. We should avoid using it.

for   against

6

Sometimes there are other options besides plastic that we can use, which decompose more quickly, like paper or bamboo.

for   against

2   Which point of view do you agree with most? Write the number here:

Explain your answer. ....

....

> 4.4 How can we tell people about plastic pollution in the oceans?

Learning goals		
Our learning goals	**I think**	**My teacher thinks**
I can identify what tasks each group member will do in order to achieve our goal.	★ ☺ ☹	★ ☺ ☹ ....
I can work well with other group members to achieve our group's goal.	★ ☺ ☹	★ ☺ ☹ ....

How can we work together to plan our role play?

1   You are going to work with your group to perform a **role play** to tell other children about looking after the oceans.

Zara's class are thinking about their role play. They want to start their preparation by thinking about what they have found out so far in their project. They have written a list of questions to help them remember.

role play

1   What is so special about the oceans?   ☐

2   What is the issue?   ☐

3   Why is it a problem?   ☐

4   Who has caused the problem?   ☐

5   How does plastic get into the oceans?   ☐

6   What can we do about it?   ☐

Some children in Zara's class wrote notes to answer the questions. Work with a partner to match each answer to the correct question by writing the letter a–f in the correct boxes.

a   Reduce, reuse, recycle.

b   Humans make plastic – throw it away without thinking.

c   A lot of it gets blown into rivers and oceans by the wind.

d   Plastic pollution in the oceans.

e   There is so much – it doesn't decompose, harms sea creatures and the environment.

f   They cover so much of the planet – amazing wildlife – plants in the oceans make oxygen which we need to breathe.

🎧 6   **2**   Zara's group talk about how they can plan a role play to show the rest of their class what they have found out about plastic pollution in the oceans. They want it to be like a TV show, where a presenter interviews guests to find out information and opinions.

Listen to what they say. Then answer these questions with your partner.

a   What are the children in Zara's group going to do first?

b   Give four examples of **roles** that they suggest.

c   How will they finish their role play?

d   Will they practise their role play?

> role

3   Arun has a good idea. He suggests that they could make some role cards for different roles that they could include in their role play.

1

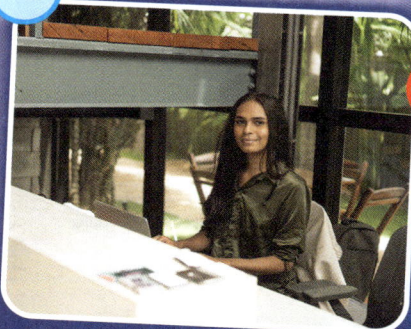

Name: Luana

Job: Manager of a hotel by a lovely beach

Opinion: All the plastic on the beach will stop visitors coming to the hotel.

2

Name: Gorka

Job: Organises wildlife-watching boat trips

Opinion: People pay to see whales and dolphins, not lots of rubbish.

3

Name: Hadiza

Job: Catches fish on a large trawler

Opinion: A few bits of old fishing equipment won't make any difference in a huge ocean.

With your partner, think of two more characters you could use in your role play. They could be characters you have been introduced to in this project, or you could make up your own. Make role play cards for them.

4

Name:

Job:

Opinion:

5

Name:

Job:

Opinion:

Top tip

You can get ideas for more characters by looking at the points of view on page 137. You can make up names and draw pictures of your characters too.

4 Now decide with your group which characters will be in your role play. You can choose the characters that Arun's group suggested, or new characters that you and your group members have made up.

You will need to include:

- the TV presenter, who doesn't give an opinion
- a character who is an **expert** and can explain why oceans are important
- at least one character who is worried about plastic pollution
- at least one character who has a different point of view.

You may want to include:

- a character with an idea about how to cut down on plastic pollution
- another character with an opinion for or against plastic.

Write the name of each group member next to the type of character they will play in your role play:

Name of group member	Character role	Character name
....	TV presenter	....
....	Expert Character	....
....	First point of view	....
....	Second point of view	....
....	Third point of view	....
....	Solution to problem	....

expert

Did you know?

What has three hearts, blue blood, a doughnut-shaped brain and eight arms? An octopus, of course! Their large brain means they are very good at working out puzzles and solving problems, too.

How can we make our role play successful?

Zara's group have started making a plan for their role play.

Name of our TV show: Let's Talk on Tuesdays

Running order	What will they talk about?
1 Presenter	Welcome the audience
2 Presenter + Lucas	Say how plastic harms sea creatures (dolphin protection society)

They have thought of a name for their TV show. They have started to work out the 'running order' – the order in which the different people will speak.

running order

1   With your group, make your own plan. Think about:

- what your TV show will be called
- the best order for the different people to speak
- what each person will talk about
- how the presenter will open and close the show, and what questions to ask the guests.

2   Once you have made your group plan, start planning what your own character will say. Make sure you know what their ideas about plastic pollution are – you can use things they said in earlier lessons. Check with your group that what you will say fits in with what the presenter and other characters will say.

Did you know?

Did you know that the manta ray is one of the largest fish in the ocean? It can weigh over 1,000 kg and, with its wings spread, it can be up to seven metres wide. However, despite its enormous size, the manta ray is completely harmless to humans.

> 4.5 How will we perform our role play to an audience?

Learning goals		
Our learning goals	I think	My teacher thinks
I can talk about an issue clearly.	★ ☺ 😐	★ ☺ 😐 ....
I can ask questions and suggest ideas in a class discussion.	★ ☺ 😐	★ ☺ 😐 ....

Top tip

Don't worry if things aren't perfect. A practice performance is a good opportunity to make your presentation even better. It will work best if everyone works well together.

How can we get ready for our role play?

1   Think about the plan your group has made.
Talk about these questions together:

- Did you make any changes to your plan?

- How will your planning make your role play even better?

2   Now you are ready to practise performing your role play.
You could do this more than once if you have the time.

How can we watch each other's role plays?

1   Take it in turns to perform your role plays to your audience.

2   Watch each group's performance, then talk about what other groups' role plays show the audience about plastic pollution in the oceans.

As you watch, complete this form.

Group role play review

Name of group members:

....

Did the role play have:

- an expert character who explained what the problem was?   Yes / No
- characters who had different opinions?   Yes / No
- suggestions for actions people could do to reduce plastic pollution?   Yes / No
- a TV presenter who asked good questions?   Yes / No

3 After you watch, ask the group a question.
   Is there something you would like to know more about?

4 How could the group make their role play even better?
   Make one or two suggestions politely.

Have you thought about...

Maybe it would be better if you...

Do you think it would be better if...

〉 4.6 What have we learned during this project?

Learning goals		
Our learning goals	**I think**	**My teacher thinks**
I can talk about ways I have worked well in my group.	★ ☺ 😐	★ ☺ 😐 ....
I can describe something I could do better in my group next time.	★ ☺ 😐	★ ☺ 😐 ....
I can talk about something I have learned that has changed my point of view.		

How well did I work in my group?

Sofia and Arun are reflecting on the work they have done for their group's role play. They talk about how their group decided what information and characters they needed to help them explain the problem of plastic pollution in the oceans.

Zara's character asked the others some great questions. This really helped our audience to understand about the problem with single-use plastics.

I should have made my character say a bit more about how long plastic takes to decompose.

1 Think about your group's role play and answer these questions.

The character I played in our role play was ....

Something I did well in our role play ....

....

A good idea I had...

....

How I helped other people in my group to plan our role play

....

2 Arun thinks the character he was pretending to be could have explained something more clearly if he did the role play again. What do you think you could do better next time?

Something I would like to do better next time ....

....

Next time, I hope to ....

....

This will help my group because ....

....

3 Work with your group. Think about all the activities you have completed together. Talk about the things you did to help each other, then answer the questions.

a What helpful thing did each person in the group do to help prepare and perform your role play?

Name	How they helped
....	....
....	....
....	....
....	....
....	....

b   How well did the group work together?   ★   ☺   😐

c   Do you think your group was successful in your task to tell other children about looking after the oceans?   ★   ☺   😐

Explain your reason: ....

What can we tell each other about what we have learned?

Talk with a partner from your group.

Ask them to look at these statements and (circle) the best symbol for you.

How well does your partner think that you:

Listened to others in the group?   ★   ☺   😐

Made some helpful suggestions?   ★   ☺   😐

Helped the group to agree?   ★   ☺   😐

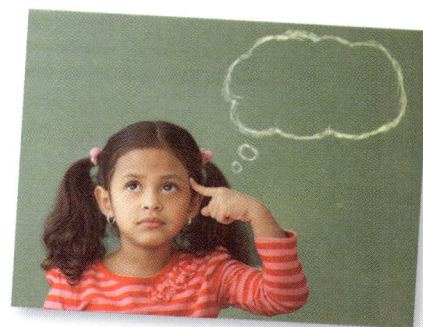

What have I found out that makes me think differently about using plastic?

Marcus and Zara are reflecting on the work they have done on their project about plastic pollution in the oceans.

They remember what they used to think about using plastic, what they learned during the project and how they feel about it now.

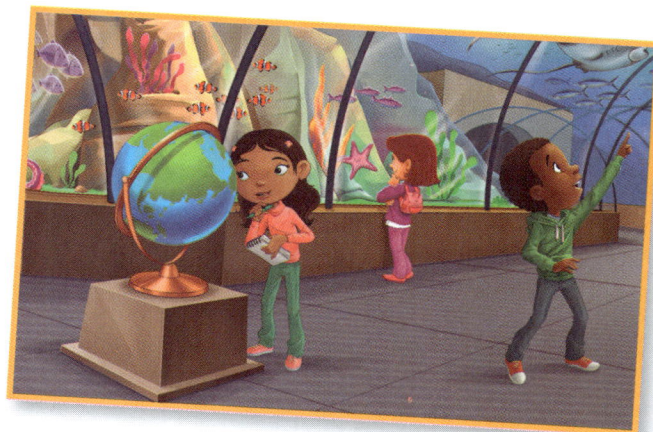

I didn't know there was so much pollution in the oceans. Now I'm going to try not to use single-use plastic.

I didn't know it floated down rivers to the sea. If I see plastic on the ground, I'll put it in a bin.

Now reflect on what you have learned and how you feel about the issue after learning about it.

1   Think about something you have found out that you didn't know before.

Plastic is a problem because: ....

I can help to cut down on the amount of plastic that ends up

in the oceans by: ....

2   Think about something you learned from an activity in this project.
    Say what the activity was and explain how it helped you learn.

    Something I learned from an activity ....

What have we learned?

Now look back over your learning goals in this project and finish
these sentences:

In this project I learned how to ....

....

Something I did well in this project was ....

....

Next time I want to learn how to ....

....

Glossary

affect	to change something or someone
axis	a line at the side or bottom of a graph that shows numbers or the type of data being measured
bar chart	a mathematical picture that shows different amounts using rectangles with different heights or lengths
blurb	a short description that makes people interested in a book or product
carbohydrate	a type of food that gives the body energy
Carroll diagram	a table used in mathematics to sort objects, numbers and shapes by what they have in common
chain reaction	a series of events where each one causes the next one to happen
column	any block of numbers or words written one under the other
conclusion	the final part of something
courier	a person or company that takes messages, letters or parcels from one person or place to another
crop	to cut down a computer image so that it is the size you want
current	moving areas of water that flow like rivers through the ocean
data	information, especially facts or numbers, collected to help decision-making
decompose	to break down naturally

draft	write some text that you will work on again later
environment	the air, water and land where people, animals and plants live
exhaust	the waste gas from a car
expert	someone who knows a lot about a subject
fat	a type of food that gives the body energy, but if not all used up, it is stored inside the body; it helps keep important body parts healthy
food group	food is grouped into different sets – like protein, carbohydrates, fat or vitamins and minerals
frequency table	an arrangement of numbers into rows to show how often something happens
get stuck in traffic	when a vehicle cannot move, or can only move slowly, because the route is very full of other vehicles
ghost gear	rubbish thrown in the sea from fishing boats, like old plastic nets and ropes
GPS map	a world-wide system of satellites and computers that makes a picture showing where landmarks like countries, towns, roads and rivers are
hobby	an activity that you enjoy and do for fun
horizontal	flat along the ground or the bottom of a page
hydrated	having enough liquid inside our bodies to stay healthy
improve	to make something better
information panel	a display of facts about a situation, person or event
junk food	foods that are unhealthy but quick and easy to eat, containing a lot of fat, sugar or salt

key	a list of the symbols used in a map or book with explanations of what they mean
landfill site	a place where rubbish is taken to be stored
lifelong learning	getting knowledge, understanding and skills throughout a person's whole life
local	from or connected with a particular area
marine	to do with the sea
nutritious	a word that describes the types of foods that give us energy, help us grow and keep our bodies working properly
oxygen	a gas with no smell or colour that forms a large part of the air on Earth, and is needed by animals and plants to live
pictogram	a picture or symbol that represents a word, phrase or idea
pie chart	a way of showing how a total amount is divided up by separating a circle into parts
pollution	when air, land or water is damaged by harmful products or rubbish
proportion	a part of a total number or amount
protein	a type of food that the body needs for growth and repair
public transport	buses, trains and even boats used to move lots of people around at once
purpose	why you do something or why something exists
qualification	an official record showing that you have finished a training course or have the necessary skills
reduce	to make something less

reflect	to think carefully, especially about possibilities and opinions
relevant	related or useful to what is happening or being talked about
role	the position or purpose that someone or something has to do
role model	someone you try to behave like because you admire them
role play	to pretend to be a particular character and to behave and react as they would
row	blocks of numbers or words written one next to another, in a straight line
rubbish	waste material or things that are no longer wanted or needed
running order	the arrangement of items in a presentation or show so that it makes sense
survey	an examination of people's opinions or behaviour made by asking people questions
sustainable	ways of doing things that do not harm the environment
tally	a record or count of a number of things
vertical	pointing straight up, either straight up from the ground, or from bottom to top of your paper
vitamins and minerals	substances in food that helps to keep the body healthy and working

Acknowledgements

The authors and publishers acknowledge the following sources of copyright material and are grateful for the permissions granted. While every effort has been made, it has not always been possible to identify the sources of all the material used, or to trace all copyright holders. If any omissions are brought to our notice, we will be happy to include the appropriate acknowledgements on reprinting.

Thanks to the following for permission to reproduce images:

Unit 1 Nurphoto/GI; FG Trade Latin/GI; Ljubaphoto/GI; Kali9/GI; Tara Moore/GI; Orientfootage/GI; SDI Productions/GI; Craigrjd/GI; Richard Newstead/GI; J Morrill Photo/GI; SDI Productions/GI; Victor/GI(x2); Fly View Productions/GI; Tim Platt/GI; Jupiterimages/GI; Andersen Ross Photography Inc/GI; Solstock/GI; Fly View Productions/GI; **Unit 1 Video** Chuck And Sarah Fishbein/GI; Stock KM/GI; Great Jones Productions/GI; FG Trade Latin/GI; Bloomberg/GI; Ljubaphoto/GI; Kali9/GI; Petroglyphfilms/GI; Tara Moore/GI; Eakgrunge/GI; Orientfootage/GI; **Unit 2** Kupicoo/GI; Mike Kemp/GI; Catherine Delahaye/GI; Kzenon/GI; Deepak Sethi/GI; Zhonghui Bao/GI; Lorado/GI; Lisegagne/GI; Elena Danileiko/GI; Spxchrome/GI; Cako74/GI; Busra İspir/GI; Jorn Georg Tomter/GI; Sean Locke/GI; BSPC/GI; Berit Myrekrok/GI; Cpuga/GI; Fatcamera/GI; Douglas Freer/GI; Portishead1/GI; Xixinxing/GI; Chud/GI; Cnythzl/GI; Tatiana Maksimova/GI; Weekend Images Inc/GI; Lauren Burke/GI; Jack Andersen/GI; Anna Efetova/GI; Jose Luis Pelaez Inc/GI; Ariel Skelley/GI; Fatcamera/GI; **Unit 2 Video** Microstockhub/GI; Sayoesso/GI; Peathegee Inc/GI; ITN/GI; Solstock/GI; Energy Films Library/GI; BSPC/GI; Alatriste1/GI; Alvarez/GI; Dennis Welsh/GI; **Unit 3** Fatcamera/GI; Thana Prasongsin/GI; Yagi Studio/GI; Michael H/GI; Dorling Kindersley/GI; Jayk7/GI; Calvindexter/GI; Whitebalance.Oatt/GI; Lechatnoir/GI; Maskot/GI; Mark Andersen/GI; Heath Korvola/GI; Goodboy Picture Company/GI; Tetra Images/GI; Kimberrywood/GI; Inti St Clair/GI; Carol Yepes/GI; SDI Productions/GI; John Slater/GI; Marc Romanelli/GI; Kali9/GI; **Unit 3 Video** Whitebalance.Oatt/GI; Annick Vanderschelden Photography/GI; Fatcamera/GI; Simonkr/GI(x2); FG Trade/GI; Cinoby/GI; Placebo365/GI; Photolibrary Pty Limited/GI(x2); Imazins/GI; NBC News Archives/GI; Sky News/GI; Armand Burger/GI; Stockerthings/GI; Konmesa/GI; Darrenwise/GI; ITN/GI; Placebo365/GI; **Unit 4** Sinology/GI; Martin Ruegner/GI; Philip Thurston/GI; Peter Dazeley/GI; Johngollop/GI; Donot6/GI; Kyoshino/GI; Popovaphoto/GI; Winai Tepsuttinun/GI; Peter Dazeley/GI(x2); Mensent Photography/GI; Chanuth/GI; Pepifoto/GI; Srinophan69/GI; Mint Images/GI; Grigorii Galasuk/GI; Citizens Of The Planet/GI; Johner Images/GI; Mesquitafms/GI; Takir Ibrahim/GI; Peter Cade/GI; Milan Jovic/GI; Brian Kennedy/GI; Greg Schneider/GI; Rosemary Calvert/GI; Pipat Wongsawang/GI; Reinhard Dirscherl/GI; Hugh Hastings/GI; Ibrahim Suha Derbent/GI; Doble-D/GI; Matteo Colombo/GI; Alistair Berg/GI; Mesquitafms/GI; Milan Jovic/GI; Hugh Hastings/GI; Simonkr/GI; Buena Vista Images/GI; James R.D. Scott/GI; Yasser Chalid/GI; Jupiterimages/GI; Fatcamera/GI; Jose Luis Pelaez Inc/GI; Richvintage/GI

Key: GI = Getty Images

Cover by Omar Aranda (Beehive Illustration)